ALSO BY ALAN D. GAFF

Amid the Ruins

From the Halls of the Montezumas

Ordered West

Blood in the Argonne

A Corporal's Story

Bayonets in the Wilderness

On Many a Bloody Field

Brave Men's Tears

If This Is War

LOU GEHRIG

The Lost Memoir

ALAN D. GAFF

Simon & Schuster

NEW YORK   LONDON   TORONTO
SYDNEY   NEW DELHI

Simon & Schuster
1230 Avenue of the Americas
New York, NY 10020

First Simon & Schuster hardcover edition May 2020

SIMON & SCHUSTER and colophon are registered trademarks
of Simon & Schuster, Inc.

For information about special discounts for bulk purchases,
please contact Simon & Schuster Special Sales at 1-866-506-1949
or business@simonandschuster.com.

The Simon & Schuster Speakers Bureau can bring authors to your
live event. For more information or to book an event, contact the
Simon & Schuster Speakers Bureau at 1-866-248-3049
or visit our website at www.simonspeakers.com.

Interior design by Paul Dippolito

Manufactured in the United States of America

1   3   5   7   9   10   8   6   4   2

Library of Congress Cataloging-in-Publication Data
Names: Gehrig, Lou, 1903–1941, author. | Gaff, Alan D., editor, writer of introduction,
writer of additional commentary.
Title: The lost memoir / Lou Gehrig, Alan D. Gaff.
Description: First Simon & Schuster hardcover edition. | New York : Simon & Schuster, 2020. |
"Portions of this text were previously published in 1927 by the *Oakland Tribune* as *Following the
Babe.*" | Includes bibliographical references and index.
Identifiers: LCCN 2019033015 (print) | LCCN 2019033016 (ebook) |
ISBN 9781982132392 (hardcover) | ISBN 9781982132415 (ebook)
Subjects: LCSH: Gehrig, Lou, 1903-1941. | New York Yankees (Baseball team) | Baseball
players—United States—Biography. | Baseball—United States—History—20th century.
Classification: LCC GV865.G4 A3 2020 (print) | LCC GV865.G4 (ebook) |
DDC 796.357092 [B]—dc23

LC record available at https://lccn.loc.gov/2019033015
LC ebook record available at https://lccn.loc.gov/2019033016

ISBN 978-1-9821-3239-2
ISBN 978-1-9821-3241-5 (ebook)

Endpapers: Getty Images

To Cathy Arnoldy Swisher
World Champion Frog Leg Smuggler

Contents

Introduction

Throughout the 1920s, Lou Gehrig was one of the most famous men in the country. He was cementing his reputation as a baseball player of true greatness. Lou, "the Iron Horse," showed up every day and played his heart out. His gentle charm and home run hitting made him a star at a time when the country was hungry for them. The Roaring Twenties positioned baseball at the heart of the nation's collective consciousness, and the Yankees were at the top of the American League. In the seven years since Babe Ruth had joined the team in 1920, they had finished first four times and had won the 1923 World Series.

American society following World War I had been transformed. A modern world awaited. Sensationalist newspapers stuffed with game play photographs exploded in popularity. Radio broadcasts that aired sporting events in addition to news, music, and variety shows expanded across the country. This was an era of ostentatious displays of individualism. It seemed as though everyone wanted to contend for fame and recognition. Men and women went to extraordinary lengths to set records, especially in sporting contests.

Sports fandom was shifting toward a glorification of individual players and their statistics. This intersection of sports reporting with a hero worship of athletes presented opportunities for entrepreneurs to step forward. The pioneering sports agent Christy Walsh led the way. Walsh had failed as a cartoonist and advertising executive, but hit the big time in 1921 when he became Babe Ruth's agent.

In this new age of celebrity, fans wanted a peek into the lives of their sports heroes. To satisfy this desire, Walsh invented a new way for readers around the country to follow their favorites without actually attending games. On March 19, 1921, he announced the formation of the Christy Walsh Syndicate. While Walsh would manage every aspect of Babe Ruth's finances, his specialty was selling newspaper columns under the bylines of famous athletes. Eschewing game coverage, he formed a stable of ghostwriters, employing some of the most notable sportswriters of the day, to write and sell columns and sports memoirs to newspapers across the country. Walsh concentrated on signing personalities and journalists who could churn out material in the fields of boxing, football, and baseball, with the athlete, the ghostwriter, and him sharing the revenue.

The Christy Walsh Syndicate had a powerful influence on America's sports pages. Ruth, Ty Cobb, and Walter Johnson flooded the nation with memoirs in the form of newspaper columns. In 1927, Walsh saw a chance to capitalize on another star. He set out to profit from a relative newcomer to the New York Yankees by inking an agreement for young Lou to furnish a memoir of his baseball life.

All that year, Gehrig had been in what was styled as a home run derby with his teammate Babe Ruth. Since hitting fifty-four homers in 1920, an extraordinary total because the player in second place hit only nineteen, Babe's prodigious blasts had lured fans to the ballparks in droves. Until Gehrig emerged as a serious competitor, no one had stepped forward to challenge Babe. Christy Walsh framed this as a modern David versus Goliath baseball story. Christy predicted that a memoir written by Lou would be an immediate hit.

Gehrig was a different type of player. He didn't share the boisterous personality of his legendary counterpart Babe Ruth. One interviewer wrote of Lou, "He was simply a very ordinary, good human being; a man whose only inheritance was unusual physical strength, a capacity for hard work, a willingness to sacrifice and learn." Lou was never a showman and had no intention of becoming one. He shunned the limelight. Family, especially his mother, meant everything to him, more than any laurel. A modest and shy gentleman, Lou enjoyed being alone—taking long walks, riding roller coasters for hours, reading anything from Tolstoy to the funny papers, and playing with his dog.

Given that New York City was saturated with coverage of the Yankees and Babe Ruth, Walsh looked farther west and contracted with the *Oakland Tribune* and the *Pittsburgh Press* for Lou Gehrig to pen his life story, which would subsequently also appear in the *Ottawa Daily Citizen* in Canada. Lou's memoir ran serially under the title *Following the Babe*, since he hit in the cleanup position behind Ruth in the Yankees' lineup.

Most famous athletes talked with sportswriters who acted as ghostwriters, turning their conversations into entertaining newspaper columns. So it is likely Lou had some help with his series. Sportswriter Ford Frick would claim that he assisted Lou in writing his 1927 World Series columns, but never professed to helping with *Following the Babe*. No matter who wrote down the words, there is no doubt that Lou's memoir came directly from the heart.

The *Oakland Tribune* proclaimed: "For the past decade, every boy in America has dreamed of being a second Babe Ruth—few daring to voice aloud such a fairy-tale ambition—and none, save one, attaining even the remotest approach to the King of Swat-dom. But that one, 'Columbia Lou' Gehrig, in the space of three short years, has swatted his way from the sandlots of New York to the very bailiwick of the mighty Babe!" Editors promoted the in-spirational angle of Lou's story: "Gehrig tells his story of dreams come true—high school victories, college glory, and big league fame—in a manner that will inspire every boy and parent in the land."

Tribune readers learned of the impending serial on August 10, 1927, when a photo of Lou and "Ma" Gehrig appeared in the sports section. Lou—hair immaculately groomed, dressed in white shirt and bow tie, and wearing an apron—appears to be helping his mom dry dishes in the family kitchen. A caption noted that when not assisting his mother and "not hitting home runs or otherwise disturbing the peace of mind of rival pitchers, he is kept busy preparing articles for *Tribune* readers."

Following the Babe appeared on August 18, with plans for thirty installments. All went as scheduled until late that month when the newspaper admitted, "Lou Gehrig has been so busy trying to catch up to Babe Ruth that he is late with this week's installment of his life history." On the thirty-first, editors announced, "According to word received today, Lou will not have another chapter ready until next week, and then his story will appear only three times a week instead of daily." Two days later, they proclaimed that Lou was "back on the job again," along with a news flash that the famous slugger would provide articles on the upcoming World Series. All went according to plan until mid-September, when Gehrig's articles began to appear out of order and one just disappeared, leaving his life story one short of the projected thirty chapters. To meet his looming deadlines, Walsh arranged for sportswriter Ford Frick to assist Lou in writing his World Series columns.

Lou Gehrig's memoir was then forgotten, buried in the mists of time, and largely overlooked by baseball historians and Gehrig biographers. When I discovered these columns while researching another topic, there was no doubt they needed to be brought to the public's attention. This sensational discovery is a unique opportunity for the world to be reintroduced to one of its most famous sportsmen. Told in Gehrig's voice, these stories will transport fans to a bygone era of baseball. Readers will learn of his upbringing and struggles as he learned to hit and field in high school and college. Upon joining the Yankees in 1923, Lou stood in awe of established stars, many of whom offered advice that advanced his career. By the 1927 season, Lou Gehrig was being mentioned in the same breath as Babe Ruth, Ty Cobb, Rogers Hornsby, and Tris Speaker.

This version of *Following the Babe* has been slightly modified from its original newspaper format, with columns being consolidated into logical chapters and spelling standardized. The *Oakland Tribune's* version of *Following the Babe* has been adhered to because it's the only complete run of the three accounts. Obvious typographical errors have been corrected, and a few commas have been inserted for clarification. Except for these minor changes, this narrative is just as it was originally published during the 1927 season.

Reading Gehrig's life story ninety-three years after it first appeared is a real treat for baseball fans, whether they are Yankees lovers or not. This is a glimpse into an era peopled by men who have been forgotten or remain in the public eye only through their mythic status. Gehrig describes them all with the same gusto, whether Hall of Famers or journeymen, relating anecdotes that make long-dead ballplayers come alive. *Following the Babe* is a chatty memoir that gives fascinating insights into the greatest baseball team of all time, the 1927 Yankees, also known as Murderers' Row. It also serves as a Horatio Alger story, relating how a poor kid from Yorkville in Upper Manhattan grew up to become a world-famous athlete.

Lou's love for baseball is infectious. As he once described his connection to the game, "The smack of a ball in a fielder's glove, the crack of a bat against the horsehide, and immediately the *game* gets me. The crowds, the color, the feeling of expectancy, the umpire with his mask and chest pad, the windup of the pitcher, a fast throw, a slide for base . . . the whole thing, and every bit of it gives me a thrill."

His records speak for themselves: American League Most Valuable Player Awards in 1927 and 1936; Triple Crown winner in 1934; *Sporting News* Most Valuable Player Awards in 1931, 1934, and 1936; enshrinement in the National Baseball Hall of Fame in 1939. Lou won the nickname the Iron Horse for playing in 2,130 consecutive major-league games, a record that would stand until 1995.

Lou Gehrig's remarkable achievements came not from a God-given natural talent but from a dogged determination to better himself and a passionate love for the game. In Gehrig's mind, there was no substitute for hard work. He devoted every day of his life to self-improvement. Noted for his strength and stamina, he resonated with fans on an unusually personal level, in the words of Jack Sher, "immortal because somehow he managed to touch and soften the heart of everyone who heard his name."

There is a real poignancy to this tale. Six feet tall, with the legs and arms of a heavyweight boxer, Lou was one of the most powerful men to ever play the game. Sadly, he is now remembered more for his premature death than for his storybook career. In 1939 Lou was diagnosed with amyotrophic lateral sclerosis, a degenerative neuromuscular disorder that slowly robbed him of his famed strength. That malady is now commonly known as Lou Gehrig's disease. After wasting away for two years, Lou drew his last breath on June 2, 1941, seventeen days short of his thirty-eighth birthday. When Lou Gehrig died, something beautiful left this world. His memoir stops with the conclusion of the Yankees' 1927 World Series win. The brevity of the story makes it all the more powerful. A biographical essay by me follows Lou's memoir, adding context and depth.

His tragically brief life has been immortalized in the classic 1942 film *The Pride of the Yankees*, with Gary Cooper starring as the Hall of Fame slugger and reenacting Gehrig's famous speech in which he confessed, "I consider myself the luckiest man on the face of the earth." Now it is our turn to be the lucky ones, reliving the exploits of a young, vibrant ballplayer as he again steps to the plate and begins *Following the Babe*.

—Alan D. Gaff, July 2019

The Lost Memoir

Chapter 1

I guess every youngster who ever tossed a ball or swung a bat has dreams of some day breaking into big league baseball. I know I did.

Up around Harlem, where I was born, there were dozens of "kid teams" playing on the street corners and vacant lots. None of the boys had uniforms, and not many of them even had gloves. And whenever they staged a game, they had to post sentries on the corners to watch for cops. It was against the law to play ball in the streets. But we had a lot of fun.

The Giants were the big show in New York in those days, and all of us dreamed of growing up and joining the Giants. Benny Kauff and Davey Robertson were our heroes. And George Burns. We used to stand outside the gate at the Polo Grounds and watch the players come out after the game. And the first real baseball thrill I ever had was one afternoon when Davey Robertson tossed an old baseball into the crowd, and I managed to grab it. For the next week, I was captain of the team and going great. Then the ball was lost, and my job went with it. You had to have either a ball or a bat if you wanted to be a captain of a team in those days.

I suppose I played on a dozen different kid teams. And not

very long on any of them. I was too fat. The boys used to call me "Fatty," and in our one ol' cat and cross-out games,* they'd throw the ball wide to me just to get a good laugh when I started to waddle after it. Believe me, it's no joke to be the little fat boy of the neighborhood. I never was much of a fighter, but I guess I had more fights over being called "Fatty" than from all other causes put together.

I'll never forget it.

Only the other day outside the Stadium, there was a kid game in progress, and I stood there watching one youngster who was so round that he puffed and panted every time he stopped to pick up a ball. The other boys were kidding him, and he was half in tears, but he stayed with it.

"Poor little cuss," I thought, "I know just how you feel." For it was the same sort of kidding I had to stand for when I was his age.

Being kidded so much made me shy about baseball, too, and even my dreams of the big leagues were buried in layers of excess weight. I suppose I would have outgrown the whole baseball idea, but a boy friend of mine, Willie Contente, told Coach DuSchatko of Commerce High School that I could play ball. The coach ordered me out for practice. For two weeks, I hesitated about going. I was afraid I would be kidded. I was fearful that I wouldn't make good. I dreamed a thousand dreams of playing—and all of those nightmares.

---

* Town ball was an early form of baseball with a variety of rules. A game with eight or fewer players on a side was called cat. Cross-out was a play by the fielding team when a ball was thrown across the path of the base runner.

But the coach kept after me. And finally, I screwed up enough courage to go over to the gym and report. The coach looked me over from head to foot, and a bit doubtfully, too.

"H-m-m," he said, "you'll have to get rid of a lot of that fat if you ever expect to play baseball!"

But he gave me a uniform. And that afternoon, I stepped out on the diamond in a real baseball uniform for the first time in my life.

Talk about thrills!

Hitting a home run with the bases full never gave me a greater kick than I got that day when I put on a real baseball uniform for the first time and went out for my first real workout on a smooth and well-kept diamond.

As a high school ballplayer, I was no bargain.

The coach put me in the outfield first, and I chased fly balls all over the lot. But it's a matter of record that I never caught up with one! He tried me out as a pitcher, and I looked better there, but I was too wild to do any good.

Finally, I got moved to first base. And I managed to hold that job—largely because we were badly in need of infielders, and I could hold on to a ball when it was thrown my way.

As a hitter, I was a bust. During that first year I played for Commerce High School, I had a batting average of .170, and I don't believe I hit half a dozen balls out of the infield. But the coach kept me at it all the time, and finally in 1920 I got going pretty good.

Commerce won the city championship that year, and we went out to Chicago to tackle Lane Tech. The game was played in Cubs Park, and I never before had seen so large a crowd as packed the park to watch the two high schools fight it out that day. We had a pretty good club. Al Schacht's brother [Mike], who later had a tryout with Washington, was with us. So was Al McLaughlin, who is now playing at Syracuse. And Howard Carter, the Fordham star, who is now owned by the Cincinnati club. Fred Lindstrom of the Giants was playing shortstop for Chicago against us.

It was quite a ball game. We were a run behind in the ninth inning and had the bases full when it came my turn to bat. I hadn't had a hit all day—or anything that even looked like a hit.

Harry Kane was our coach, and I went up to him. "Harry, what shall I do?" I asked.

"Do?" he growled. "Go on up there and strike out. You couldn't hit the side of a house with a fishing pole."

I went up and shut my eyes and swung.

How I ever managed to hit that ball, I don't know, but I hit it. And it went over the right field wall for a home run. Talk about thrills, I still get one every time I think about that hit. It was some blow. Even the newspapers printed stories about it—and about the high school kid who had hit a ball as far as Babe Ruth.

That was the first time I ever had my name linked with the Babe, and the first time I had really given the Babe a serious thought. He was just coming into his own as a member of the Yankees then, and the papers were full of stories about his homers. One of the Chicago papers printed my picture alongside his, and over the picture they ran a heading which said, "Will This High School Boy Be the Next Babe Ruth?" I have that clipping yet.

But the biggest kick came after the game. We were down in the dressing room having a shower when one of the boys came over.

"Say, Lou," he said, "did you know that there was a Cub scout up in the stands when you hit that one, and he wants the Cubs to sign you up."

I got a little chesty over that and started to sputter a bit.

But Harry Kane stopped me.

"Listen, kid," he said. "You can't play big league ball on the strength of one ball hit over the fence. You better go on to school and forget about it."

The best break I ever got was when I went to Columbia and met Andy Coakley, the old Yale pitcher. And it was only chance that sent me there.

When I finished high school, I had my heart set on going to Dartmouth or Penn. A lot of fellows I knew were up at Dartmouth, and I wanted to be with them. Then they had great football and baseball teams up there, too. And argue all you please about it, the average high school kid is attracted to the college that has the best athletics.

He may not be an athlete himself, but he likes to string along with a winner. A lot of college presidents have another idea, but if a mere ballplayer may be pardoned for having an opinion on educational matters, I still think that there's nothing that attracts students so much as winning teams and the publicity they get.

As I said above, I had my heart set on either Dartmouth or Penn. But my mother wasn't very well, and she didn't want me to go away from home. So we finally agreed that I would go to Columbia instead. And I enrolled for a liberal arts course, with the intention of entering either the School of Business or Civil Engineering when I had finished.

Walter Koppisch and Ben Roderick were the big men at Columbia then. Both of them were football stars, and they interested me in football. I played one season, but somehow I couldn't get the same kick out of football that I did from baseball, and during my years at Columbia, I put in most of my time on the diamond. Andy Coakley was our coach, and he knew what it was all about. He was the first man to really teach me something about hitting. And believe me, he had a hard job. In two seasons, he changed my whole style.

One day he took me down to the Yankee Stadium. It was the first time I had ever seen the Babe play. And when I saw the way he swung, watched the perfect rhythm and saw how he managed to get his full weight back of the blow without hitching or losing any of his smoothness, I made up my mind that there was the one man to pattern after. I learned a lot from Babe Ruth in that one day. And I'm still learning. Talk all you please about Cobb and Speaker and the rest of the great hitters, the Babe is in a class by himself.

Up until the moment I saw the Babe in that game, I had never had any great interest in the Yankees. As a kid, I barely knew they existed. Back in the day when a quarter was a fortune and we had to save for weeks to get the price of a bleacher seat, the Giants had been our favorites. And our quarters had all gone for a seat in the left field bleachers—"the George Burns bleachers," we always called them in the good old days. But one peep at the Babe in action made me a Yankee fan. And then and there I began dreaming of the day when I might get a tryout on the same team. And then and there I set up the Babe as my hitting model.

When I reported for practice the next day, I changed my whole batting style, with Coakley helping me. Before that, I had been a "choke" hitter, as they call a fellow who grabs the bat up toward the middle. Now I started gripping my bat at the end and taking a full-arm cut. "You've got great shoulders and great driving power," Coakley used to tell me. "If you can learn to take a full swing, you ought to be able to hit for plenty of extra bases."

I've been around college ball teams a lot, and I've talked to a good many college ballplayers. I don't believe there's a man who ever played college baseball who didn't think some time or other of making good in the big leagues. I don't mean by that that young fellows go to college for athletics alone, or that they aren't interested in their college work. But baseball has an appeal to a young fellow that can't be denied.

Then there's another thing about professional baseball that appeals to the college man. That's the opportunity it affords for making a financial stake quickly. The average chap who graduates from college with his degree as an engineer or a doctor or a lawyer faces long years of more or less privation before finally he can establish himself in his profession. Baseball offers him a quick return and the chance of building up a bank account which will enable him to tide himself over the lean years.

Men of the caliber of Eddie Collins and Art Nehf are capable of success in most any profession they take up. They have been a real credit to baseball, and they would reflect just as much credit on any other business upon which they might enter.

Time was, years ago, when professional baseball was regarded as a low class employment in college circles. Professors frowned upon it. Parents who had sent their sons to college advised against it. But those times have changed—and it was college men of the type of Matty [Christy Mathewson] and Eddie Collins, of George Sisler and Art Nehf, who brought about the change.

Some of the greatest stars the game ever has known have been college men. Christy Mathewson of Bucknell and Eddie Collins of Columbia were the pioneers. They blazed the trail, and those who followed them have kept up the tradition of high class sportsmanship. George Sisler is a Michigan University graduate. Eppa Rixey is a college man. Frank Frisch stepped right from the Fordham campus to a place in the majors. Max Carey gave up his studies for the ministry to enter professional baseball.

Arthur Nehf is a qualified engineer. Eddie Farrell of the Giants was a graduate dentist from the University of Pennsylvania, and Long Cy Williams came from Notre Dame, while Holy Cross produced Joe Dugan and [Owen] Carroll of Detroit.

Joey Sewell came from the University of Alabama to the Cleveland Indians, and his brother Luke was quick to follow in his footsteps from the same college. Bibb Falk of the White Sox, Ernie Wingard of the Browns, Vic Aldridge of the Pirates, Marty Karow of the Red Sox, Earle Combs of the Yankees, Jack Coombs and Jack Barry of the old Philadelphia Athletics, Ed Reulbach and Orvie Overall of the famous old Cubs—all of these were and are college products. Ernie Nevers, pitcher for the St. Louis Browns, was a great football player before graduating from Stanford University. And Manager Miller Huggins himself is a law school graduate.

And they are only a few of the hundreds who have stepped from the campus to the big leagues. They bettered themselves and helped baseball. And, what's more, they did not injure their college when they made the jump.

Twenty years ago, old timers tell me, educated people looked upon professional baseball as a rather off-color profession. They don't consider it so today. I believe I am typical of the college men in baseball. I went from the campus to the big league diamond. I'm still proud of my college, proud to be a college man, and proud of my membership in Phi Delta Theta. But I'm just as proud of my professional baseball connection. So are all the others. And I think that most of us, if we had it all to do over, would do again just as we did. Baseball is a great game, and worthy of the greatest and best men who ever played it.

Chapter 2

Fate and not any planning of mine sent me to the Yankees.

Some people criticized me for quitting college before graduation to go into professional baseball. I didn't want to do it. No kid ever wanted to finish a college course more than I did. And no kid's mother ever felt more badly than mine when I finally gave up college.

Here's the story: In 1920 my father was taken seriously ill. My mother had to shoulder the burden of caring for the family. It was a tough job, but she insisted on doing it while I finished school. Then in 1923 Mother was taken ill with pneumonia.

There was no money coming in, and there were plenty of expenses to meet. It was up to me. I had to get a job. And I had to have a job where the pay would be enough to take care of my family. Baseball was my best bet.

The Athletics had been after me. So had Washington. But I had seen the Babe hit one and was a Yankee fan. I wanted to get with the Yankees, and Andy Coakley wanted me to.

Frankly, I didn't have any idea I could make good in big league baseball. Even when I began getting letters from the various clubs, I figured that I wasn't good enough for professional baseball. And when I decided to sign a contract, my whole idea was that there was a chance to get some ready money to tide us over the rough spots. "I'll get some money for signing," I thought, "and then I'll get paid for the few weeks I'm with the club before they find out my weak spots. That will give me enough to meet our present expenses, and after that I can get a job downtown." I still had the idea of working for a time until my father was well, and then going back to college again.

I'll never forget the night I went home and told my mother that I was going to quit college and go into baseball. She was sick in bed, and she broke down and cried when I told her. She insisted that I should stay on in school.

"I'll be well again soon," she said, "and then everything will be all right."

Like me, she didn't think I could make good in baseball, and she was afraid that I would be let out in a few weeks, and then I'd be out of college as well as out of a job, too. It was a tough spot!

But we had to have an income, and I was the only one to earn it. I talked it over with Mother for a whole afternoon. Still she wouldn't consent. So the next day, we talked again. And finally, when she saw that I was determined to do something to earn money and that I was all set to quit school temporarily at least, then she gave her consent.

I went back to the campus and told the boys at the fraternity house that I was quitting and going into baseball. They were great to me. Some of them even wanted to loan me, money so I could keep on with my college work. And they all wished me the best luck in the world in the big leagues. All of them thought I would make good—which was more than I did at the time.

I had made up my mind. College was a thing of the past. The dream I had as a kid was about to come true. But it didn't bring half the thrill I had expected. The circumstances under which I quit college weren't pleasant, and I felt pretty badly about it.

But it was all settled. I was going to become a professional ballplayer—at least for a trial.

I'll never forget the incidents that led up to my actual signing with the Yankees. I pitched for Columbia against New York University. A lot of scouts were in the stands, but I didn't know it. I got three hits that day, including a home run over the fence. We won, 7 to 2.

After the game, we were in the showers when a little short stout chap came in. "I'm Krichell," he said. "Want to come down to the office on Monday and talk things over?"

I was sputtering under the showers and didn't know what it was all about. Andy Coakley nodded at me. "Why, yes, I guess so," I finally stammered.

After he was gone, I turned to Andy.

"Who was that fellow?" I asked.

"Why, that was Paul Krichell, the Yankee scout," Andy said. "They want you to sign right away."

Believe me, I was happy then.

On Monday I went down to the office and met Krichell and Bob Connery. Later, Ed Barrow came in and Andy Coakley. With Andy advising me, we soon arranged terms, and I signed my name to my first big league contract. Barrow told me to report at the park next day, and I went home proud as a king, with a copy of my contract to show my mother.

My biggest kick was to come next day when I went in the clubhouse. I had been in clubhouses before around in the college gyms. And I had gone around with semi-pro ballplayers when I was playing in New Jersey under the name of Long. But I had never met any real big leaguers before, and I didn't know quite what to do.

Andy Coakley went down to the clubhouse with me.

When we went in, all of the players were in there. Some of them were getting dressed. Joe Bush, Bob Meusel, Aaron Ward, and Scotty [Everett Scott] were over in one corner playing cards.

Babe Ruth was sitting on a bench right at the door, half dressed and oiling his glove. It was the closest I had ever been to him, and I guess I must have stared like a country kid getting his first look at a skyscraper. But no one paid any attention to me, and the fellows who were playing cards just looked up and said, "Hello, Andy," and went on with their game.

I guess they didn't even know I was there. It's a cinch they didn't appear to care. Andy talked to Charley O'Leary, the Yankee coach, a minute, and introduced me.

Then we went into Manager Huggins' office.

I'll never forget that first meeting with Hug in his office right off the dressing room. He was sitting down with his feet cocked up on his high desk. Andy went in first, and without taking his feet off the desk, he half turned around and shook hands with Andy.

"This is Lou Gehrig," Andy said. "He's the young fellow from Columbia I was telling you about."

"Hello, Gehrig," Hug said. "Tell Woodie to give you a uniform." Woodie, or "Doc" Woods, as he likes to be called, is the popular Yankee trainer.

And then without another word to me, Hug turned to Andy again.

"Pretty big fellow," he commented. "Is he Jewish?" Wise little Hug had his eye on the box office as well as my base hits.

I didn't wait for any more words, I just turned around, walked out of the office into the clubhouse. "Woodie" gave me a uniform, and I sat down to dress.

The boys were still playing cards. They didn't give me a tumble yet.

"Well," I thought to myself, "I'm in the big leagues now. And what was I going to do about it?"

The first day I joined the New York Yankees, I sat on the bench all through the game without a word from anyone. That great big stadium never looked so big and hopeless to me. When the game was over, Manager Huggins came over and talked to me a bit about baseball.

I'll never forget the things Hug told me.

"You're a young fellow," he said, "and I don't want you getting off on the wrong foot. Baseball in the big leagues and baseball in college is very different. You've got a lot to learn. Some of it I can tell you. Most of it you've got to find out for yourself. Don't be disappointed if the older men on this club don't seem to make a fuss over you. They have their own worries, and they can't be expected to pay a lot of attention to every kid who comes along. But you can mark this down. If you show them that you can play ball, they'll all be for you and they'll help you. Just keep your eyes and your ears open. If you want to know anything, don't be afraid to ask. And if you make a dumb play or an error, don't let it get you 'down.' Any young fellow who goes into baseball is sure to have a lot of disappointments. But just remember when things go wrong that every other man on this club has been through the same mill."

Hug took me in the clubhouse after that. He didn't introduce me to the players. He just said, "This is Lou Gehrig, fellows. He'll be with the club awhile." Notice that last word!

The Babe had taken off his uniform and was going to the showers at the time. He passed me as Hug spoke.

He stopped and held out his hand.

"H'ye, kid?" he said. If you ever heard the gruff but kindly voice of this big overgrown kid, you will appreciate what his greeting meant to me.

I shook his hand. I wanted to say something, but I couldn't think of anything to say, so I just stood and stared at him. I guess he thought I was pretty dumb. Anyhow, he never had anything more to say to me for a couple of weeks. Nor did many of the other boys, so far as that goes.

There was one funny incident, though, that happened a few days later that I will never forget.

Sam Crawford had sent Bob Meusel one of his special Crawford bats—made in four sections of wood. Babe felt it, lifted it, and said to Bob: "Let me try it?"

He took it to the plate and with his first swing lifted the ball into the bleachers. "Goodbye bat," Meusel said.

Babe continued to use the bat through the game and got four hits. Right after the game, he went into the clubhouse and immediately sent a wire to Crawford ordering a dozen of the bats sent by express immediately.

The next evening, Colonel Ruppert came into the clubhouse as the boys were dressing. I had never seen the colonel before, and I didn't know quite what to make of his visit.

The Babe spotted him when he came through the door.

"Say, Colonel," he said. "I've ordered a dozen of these Sam Crawford bats. They're $6 apiece."

The Colonel looked at Babe.

"By golly," he said, "when they come, I guess we'll have to lock them up in the safe with all the mortgages."

That is one of the stories the Babe still loves to tell. And he gets the biggest kick of all from the fact that a few days later, the umpires passed a rule forbidding him to use them, and they were all tossed out. So far as anyone knows, the Colonel is still saving them, although I imagine from the attendance figures lately his mortgages have about disappeared.

That Yankee ball club of 1923 was a wonderful organization. Real champions! As I look back on it now, I can see a lot of things that weren't perfect, and a lot of happenings that weren't entirely pleasant. But as a rookie on the bench, the whole thing struck me as being wonderful and every player a hero.

It was there on the bench in 1923 that I learned what it meant to "jockey." Jockey is the term applied to the fellows who "ride" the opposing players, and we had some great ones. The Babe, for instance, has always been a great jockey. When we're home, he's always on the field before the opposing players take their hitting practice, and he never fails to have something to say to every man who shows up. His is good-natured kidding, for the most part, and opposing players seldom get sore at the things he says. And I have never seen him sore but once, over anything other players called him. That was during the World Series of 1923.

Some of the Giants started calling him "nigger." It made him furious. It was the first time I ever really saw him lose his temper over a "riding." And when the game was over, he went into the Giant clubhouse and offered to fight anyone who cared to take a chance. Fortunately, Manager McGraw was on hand, and he smoothed things over and averted trouble. But believe me, the Babe was raging.

One of the best jockeys baseball ever knew was "Joe" Bush of "bullet" pitching fame. Joe had a loud, foghorn sort of voice that you could hear for blocks. And he used it plenty. Joe seemed to know the touchy spot of every player in the league, and he never spared any part of them. When he used to start after anyone, the rest of us would keep quiet. And if Joe really wanted to get a player's goat, he never failed. He'd do it in ten minutes.

Sam Jones was another good jockey. Like the Babe, Sam indulged in a lot of harmless kidding, and his best stunt was to keep "wise cracking" until he got the opposing player's attention. Then he'd start up a conversation and keep the other fellow talking until he didn't know what was going on out there on the field. One of his best stunts, when he was pitching, was to kid the base runners, talking to them until he got them off guard and then shooting the ball to the base to catch them flat-footed. I saw him work that three times in one series in Detroit.

The quietest man on the Yankee bench was and still is Bob Meusel. Bob seldom has a word to say. Now and then he'll grin at the kidding the other fellows are doing, but he never joins in. I suppose in the course of a month Bob won't have a dozen words to say. And he never pays any attention to what the other fellows say when he is playing, either.

Herbie Pennock is another silent one, so far as "jockeying" is concerned. Herbie is a good conversationalist, and he loves to "punch the bag" with the other players. But he doesn't jockey.

In mentioning the famous Yankee jockeys, I almost overlooked one of the very best. That was Freddy Hofmann, the catcher. Freddy was our leading jockey all the time he was with the club, and he's still at it now that he is with the Red Sox.

And so far as the other clubs are concerned, there's no man in the league who is better than Ty Cobb.

Ty's best stunt is riding the new players as they come into the league. He likes to try them out to see if they have any nerve. But if they show real stuff, there's no one in the league quicker to advise and help them than Cobb. I remember how he used to go after me when I got a few chances as a pinch hitter. Once I got a good single in a pinch but got run down between first and second. Cobb razzed me something awful. "You can sock 'em all right," he said after the inning, "but you haven't got any guts on the bases."

That made me sore. Cobb realized it immediately and kept

after me a long time afterwards about my base running and lack of "guts," which in nicer language means backbone or fighting spirit. But as several seasons passed, Cobb got tired of razzing and only recently paid me the finest compliment I ever received in baseball. But I'll let Ty tell that.

Chapter 3

The toughest news that can come to any big league rookie is the news that he is to be shipped to the minors. Or the bush leagues, as the boys call them.

Believe me, it takes the heart out of a fellow.

I suppose I never felt more discouraged in my whole life than I did in August 1923 when Miller Huggins called me into his office and told me he was sending me to the Hartford club of the Eastern League.

For a little bit, I thought of quitting baseball entirely, and if somebody had come along and offered me a job at that moment, the chances are I would have been out of baseball forever.

But nobody did—and I went to Hartford. It was the best thing that ever happened to me. And here's a tip to young ballplayers. When you get a chance to play regularly in the minors, take it. Six weeks of actually playing out there on the diamond every day is worth more than two seasons of bench warming with the best big league club that ever existed.

There's just one way to learn baseball, and that's to play it every day. I know. For I learned a lot up there at Hartford with Pat O'Connor.

As soon as I arrived, Pat put me in the game, and I was terrible. I couldn't hit the size of my hat, and the longer I played, the worse I got. Pat had about given me up and was all ready to ship me back to the Yankees, when I managed to get hold of one and broke up a ball game with a home run.

After that, he began to show more interest in me and began coaching me on a lot of inside baseball that I never even knew existed.

Pat, incidentally, gave me one bit of advice which I believe is the best I ever had anywhere.

"Listen kid," he said. "When you're playing baseball, always stay on the up and up. The baseball season is only five months long. While you're playing baseball, make baseball your business. You'll still have six months in the winter to play around all you please. You can't play baseball in the day time and run around at nights. Just save your parties and your wild times for the winter days."

That's gospel truth, too.

I'm no preacher, and I'm no saint. But as regards training, I've always been conscientious. I watch my diet carefully, I don't stay out late at night, I get up early in the morning, and during the off season in winter I exercise constantly.

Of course, training is an individual matter. Fellows like Joe Dugan or Earle Combs, for instance, need rest during the winter more than they need exercise. Their only worry about weight is to keep from losing it. But I'm inclined to put on weight easily, and taking off excess weight is a lot tougher job than putting on a little when you're under weight.

Incidentally, the Babe was the first one to give me advice about keeping in condition.

"Listen, Lou," he said to me. "Don't be a sap. Keep in condition. Don't let yourself get soft. I made a lot of mistakes when I was coming along. I didn't eat right, and I didn't live right. Later, I had to pay for all those mistakes. I don't want you to do the same thing. Just take a tip from me, and tell the 'party guys' to go sell their papers. You'll be a lot better off."

I'll never forget that advice of Babe's.

And sometimes maybe I'll have a chance to pass it on to some other rookies who come up like I did, wondering what it's all about.

I don't care who the player is or how good he may have been in the minors, he's bound to get a kick out of his first major league game. And not a pleasant one, perhaps. When I was a sophomore in college, I remember one of the seniors coming around to the fraternity house after commencement exercise. He sat down in a chair, crossed his legs, and looked for a long time at his diploma. Then he turned to the other fellows sitting in the room.

"Well," he said, holding up his diploma, "now I've got it, what am I going to do about it."

That's the feeling I had the first time I ever broke into a big league box score. I'll never forget it. It was in the fall of 1923, and Manager Huggins sent me up to pinch hit for the pitcher in a game with Washington. I was nervous as I walked to the plate, and more nervous as I stood there while the announcer gave my name to the fans.

John Hollingsworth was pitching for Washington, and he was

a fastball pitcher with a sweeping overhand motion. I had hardly stepped into the box before he wound up and sent the ball zipping right through the heart of the plate. I swung and missed. A moment later, I had struck out on three pitched balls, without getting so much as a foul.

I turned and walked back to the bench, and I never knew how long that walk could be.

"Well," I thought to myself, "I guess that was my big chance, and now I've muffed it. I'll probably be headed back to the minors tonight."

Hug didn't even look my way as I went back to the bench, and I sat down without a word. It so happened that I was alongside the Babe. He looked up and grinned as I sat down.

"Never mind, kid," he said, "You'll sock one the next time. Anyhow, you took your cuts. You didn't stand there and let 'em call 'em on you."

I didn't make any reply. I couldn't. But I guess I never appreciated anything more in the world than I did those words of the Babe's. And in one way, he was right.

The next time I did get hold of one.

It was some days later before I got a chance to hit again. This time we were playing St. Louis, and Elam Vangilder was pitching. Hug sent me to hit with a runner on second. Elam sent up a fastball, and I gritted my teeth and swung.

That time I got hold of it and bounced the ball off the right field fence for a double. The runner scored, and as I slid into second, I can remember thinking to myself, "Well, there's one they can't kid me about."

Believe me, I've never got more kick out of a hit in my life than I did out of that one—my first safe blow in the big leagues. And ever since that day, I've had a kindly feeling for Elam Vangilder. I've faced him a lot of times since then. I've made other hits off him too, and more than once he has struck me out. But I'll always regard Vangilder as my own personal pitcher. Probably he doesn't even remember the day or the game, or the occasion, or the fact that I was sent up to hit. But I do, and I'll never forget it because it was my first big league hit.

And when I came back to the bench, I was prouder than a king when Hug slapped me on the back and said, "Nice hitting, kid!"

At Columbia, we played baseball just for enjoyment. It was a game with us, and, winning or losing, we found it a real pleasure.

Once I had signed a Yankee contract and had put on a uniform, it didn't take me long to find out that baseball in the big leagues is a business. And the fellows who play it are businessmen—just as much businessmen as the merchants and lawyers and doctors who turn out to watch the games.

I had expected the ballplayers to be a good-natured lot of roughnecks, and easy going and careless. I found them instead to be much like college men in their seriousness and their conduct. I discovered that they talked in a matter of fact way about inside baseball, of which I knew nothing. Just to hear the pitchers discuss the players of other clubs and their strengths and weaknesses was a revelation.

And I found out that ballplayers, off the field and out of uniform, were much like other people. They had all their little hobbies and their personal likes and dislikes. The Babe, when I joined the club, was interested in raising chickens, and I've heard him sit in the clubhouse for a half hour at a time and discuss the various breeds, and the way of feeding and caring for chickens.

Bob Shawkey has always made a hobby of hunting. He could tell stories of deer and moose shooting that sounded like story books, and he knew and still knows more about game than any man I ever talked to.

Wallie Pipp was always interested in finance, and he and Manager Huggins used to discuss the stock market for hours at a time. There would be political discussions, too, that waxed pretty hot at times, and I was surprised to learn how closely the players followed the daily news and how great an interest they took in current events.

I guess the chief pastime of the old 1923 Yankees was cards. Everett Scott was a card shark and was always looking for a game. Mike McNally and Ernie Johnson were great card players, too, and frequently the Babe would take a hand. I had always supposed that ballplayers played poker. All the baseball stories I had read or heard always had to do with poker. But the Yankees played bridge and played it well. I guess there have been few better bridge players in the big leagues than Everett Scott and Ernie Johnson. Or anywhere else, for that matter.

Joe Dugan and Herbie Pennock, on the other hand, seldom joined in card games. Pennock has always been interested in horses and in horseback riding. He has two or three good riding horses of his own, and his greatest joy during the off season is fox hunting and riding to hounds.

Naturally, the chief topic of conversation is baseball. That is to be expected. But the chaps who hold to the old-fashioned idea that ballplayers know nothing outside their own game are wrong. When you get that notion, just remember this: Ballplayers are human, the same as fans. They have families, and wives and children, just the same as other people. They have friends, too—and outside interests. Since baseball is their business, they have to look other places for their diversion. Some of them find it in golf. Some in hunting or fishing or riding. Wallie Pipp was a steady reader. So was Waite Hoyt.

Since 1923, I've made a lot of road trips with the club, and I never yet have seen Hoyt start on a trip without at least one book in his bag. Usually he had three or four. Most folks may not realize it, but many times I've heard the newspaper men remark that Hoyt is not only one of the best-read men in baseball, but one of the best-read men they have ever known.

As one of the boys remarked, "Gene Tunney hasn't got anything on Waite Hoyt." That refers to literature, of course.

Wearing out the bench on a big league ball club day after day and wondering all the time where you'll finally end up is no joke.

When I joined the Yankees in 1923, they looked to me like the greatest ball club in the world, and the longer I sat around, the more I was impressed. I might also say depressed—from too much sitting. I thought I'd like to be an outfielder, and I'd watch Babe and Bob Meusel and Whitey Witt in every move they made. I'd see them go away back for long flies, watch them come in to take balls at their shoe strings, and sit by and marvel at the way they threw.

And the more I watched, the more depressed I got.

"I'll never be able to break in here," I figured. "Those guys are too good. Trying to beat them out of a job is a laugh."

The same went for first base. Wallie Pipp never had a better year in his life than he had in 1923. He was getting everything that came his way and hitting with the best in the business. A lot of the baseball I know now I picked up from watching Pipp. Of course, I didn't realize it at the time. But it's true.

One of the toughest jobs for a first baseman is learning to shift his feet with the throw so that he's always in position to take the throw at the shortest distance and at the same time ready to throw to another player if necessary. George Sisler gets a lot of putouts at first base that would be hits for the runner with other first basemen. He's a cat when it comes to shifting his feet. And saving a fielder six inches or a foot on a throw is often the difference between a putout and a base hit.

In those long days when I was warming the bench and wondering what it was all about, Ernie Johnson, famous utility player, was one of the best friends I had. Ernie always took an interest in kid players, and he used to get out on the infield with us and show us how to play batters, how to cover up, and how to make plays. He used to work me for hours, teaching me to shift my position and to make the throw to second base. Ernie's out in Portland, Oregon, now, and he ought to make a great manager. He certainly can teach young fellows a lot of baseball.

Feet like mine don't shift easily. They're too big. And the fellows on the bench used to kid me a lot when I'd fall all over myself trying to play first base. But they were nice about it, too.

"Say, Lou, why don't you try catching?" the Babe said to me one day. "With those dogs of yours, you could block an army at the plate!"

But even when Babe was kidding me, he was tipping me off to a lot of good baseball knowledge. Babe was one of the fellows who always figured I could hit, and he spent a lot of time showing me how to "pull" a ball to right field. I always hit to center and left, and Babe didn't like it.

"Take a tip from a guy who knows," the big fellow would say. "All those long flies you're hitting to left and center are putouts, or maybe singles and doubles. Pull 'em to right, and they're home runs.

"When you've got a mark like that right field wall to shoot at, you're a sucker if you don't do a little shooting."

And so I stood up there and swung and swung, and I went into the infield and worked and worked and worked—but all the time, I was discouraged, for I couldn't see a chance to break in with such a ball club of veterans still in their prime. All I could do was sit around with my mouth shut and my eyes and ears open. But as I began to look back, even at this early date, I couldn't offer any better advice in the world to a young man breaking into baseball than: Keep your mouth shut and your eyes and ears open.

Chapter 4

The greatest kick that comes to any young fellow breaking into the big leagues is when he makes his first real trip around the circuit. You may hang around a ball club for weeks and weeks seeing the players every afternoon on the bench, but it's not until you've lived with them and eaten with them and slept with them that you really feel you "belong."

During my college days, Tris Speaker was always my idol outside of the Yanks. In 1923 I made my first trip around the circuit, and Cleveland was our first stop. I was sitting on our bench, listening to the chatter, when Speaker happened along.

He stopped to talk to Babe, and I edged over towards them.

I guess I must have acted like a little kid wanting to get a baseball signed, for the Babe noticed me.

"What's th' matter, kid?" he asked. "Scared of this old leather neck? Guess you've got his goat, Tris," he said turning to Speaker.

"Spoke," as they called the great center fielder with the gray hair, just grinned.

"I hear you're the new kid who is going to make the Babe's record look like a Swiss cheese," he said. "I hope you do. He's getting entirely too fresh," and Spoke jabbed Babe in the ribs as he said it.

A little later, we were taking batting practice, and I happened to get hold of one. The right field wall in the Cleveland park is about 30 feet high, and I hit that ball pretty well. It hit the wall on a line and bounced back almost to second base.

"Nice hitting, kid," Speaker yelled. "That's the way to sock that ball."

It was the first encouraging word I had ever had from anyone on another club, and I'll never forget it. Tris Speaker is a friend of mine forever, for that little word. I'll always have a soft spot for "Spoke."

Another star who treated me mighty well in those early days was Eddie Collins. Eddie, like myself, came from Columbia, and he's about the most famous athlete the school ever turned out. I never had seen him or met him, but I had seen his picture so often and heard so many stories about him that I recognized him the minute he came through the dugout.

Eddie is one of the most popular men who ever put on a uniform, and he always stops to talk a bit with the visiting players. I was sitting at one end of the dugout while he talked to Sam Jones and Bob Shawkey. He looked over and spied me. I hadn't the slightest idea that he even knew who I was. But he did.

"Hello, Columbia," he said and came over and sat down.

We talked for a long time, not baseball but a variety of things. Percy Haughton had just taken over the football job at Columbia then, and Eddie was interested. He asked about Haughton, and he inquired about Walt Koppisch, and Ben Roderick, and Pease and several of the other boys—who were then the big guns in Columbia football.

And don't think Eddie didn't know his football. A lot of people have an idea that chaps like Collins think only in terms of baseball. Eddie talked football, and he talked politics. He talked about college courses too and told me that someday his two boys would enroll at Columbia.

We chatted for ten or fifteen minutes, and when he left, he shook hands. "Luck to you," he said. "The more college men we can get into this game, the better it is. Don't get discouraged if you don't get all the breaks at once, and just remember that baseball is like a course in college. You've got to do a lot of studying if you want to get a passing mark. Give my regards to Professor Stockder when you see him. And keep your head up, boy. You'll make the grade."

From that day to this, Eddie Collins has been on my list of great fellows. He's a wonder.

A lot has been written in the newspapers from time to time about a Gehrig-Cobb feud. It always gives me a laugh.

Ty Cobb is one of the fieriest ballplayers I ever saw or ever expect to see. And one of the best. Off the field, he's a soft-spoken, good-natured sort of fellow. On the field, he's a fighter who doesn't give an inch. He fights for everything, and he wants everyone to fight back.

A lot of unkind things have been written and said about Ty Cobb. Like John McGraw and other men of that type, Cobb's attitude is a challenge to the fans. He's always cock-sure of himself, and he isn't afraid to show it. Ty likes to ride young players. He got a lot of riding when he broke in to the league, and he figures everyone else should get it too. He was "on me," as they call it, from the moment I joined the club. Every time we met the Tigers, I was Ty's own special property, and the things he used to say to me out there on the diamond would have me boiling.

The tamest thing he called me was a "fresh busher," and from there he climbed upward. And he never quit. "You think you're a ballplayer," he said one day at the Stadium. "All you can do is hit that ball. If you're a ballplayer, I'm the 'King of Siam.'" And he said it in a nasty tone of voice.

Once in 1925, when I was getting in the game only now and then, I went to Huggins and asked him to get waivers on me and send me to the minors, where I could play regularly.

Cobb, then Detroit's manager, apparently heard about it. For the next time I saw him, he came over where I was.

"So you want to go to the minors do you," he opened up. "Say, listen, rookie, you'll never get away from me. I'll claim you, and when I get you, I'll send you to China, where it'll take the rest of your life to get back."

The real laugh, though, happened at Detroit one day when I was on first. Cobb came rushing over, swinging his arms and apparently calling me all sorts of names. The fans thought he was going to fight, and they began riding him all over the park. All the time, Ty stood there with his jaw stuck out, his fist clenched, and his arms swinging.

And what he was really saying all the time was this:

"Make 'em think you're sore, kid. They like it. Put on the old fighting attitude. Let 'em see you're interested in the ball game. The more fight you put into it, the better the fans like it. Double up your fists. Talk loud. Make 'em think you're going to sock somebody."

I've laughed about that a lot of times. And I laughed most when my mother got hold of the paper and read that Cobb and I had been near coming to blows.

She saved the paper to show me when I came home, and, like all mothers, she wanted me to promise her that I wouldn't get into any fights.

Cobb is one of my best boosters today. When I finally got a job as a regular, he was one of the first men in the league to congratulate me. And many times he has gone out of his way to show me little tricks in hitting and in base running—tricks that only Cobb can show.

Ty has been panned a lot. But he's a great fellow. And just remember this. When he is showing all that fight out there on the field, it's because he believes baseball should be played that way. And off the field, he's a fine fellow, affable, kindly, and as fair as they come. And if you want a real treat, get Cobb in a visiting mood sometime and listen to his wonderful ideas on raising children. Or his opinions on books, art, the stock market, or nearly any subject you choose.

He gets terribly serious if you once get him started on one of his favorite subjects, which, by the way, includes Babe Ruth. It would be surprising to many people to hear the way Ty praises Babe's all-around work. Not alone his home run hitting. Even Babe says "bunk" when anyone tells him. But getting back to my own case, Tyrus Raymond Cobb rode me plenty. And I rode him back as best I could. But right now, I consider Ty Cobb one of my best friends in baseball.

You can talk about pitchers until you're blue in the face, but when you've said everything there is to say and argued everything out to the finish, it all comes back to one man.

That's Walter Johnson.

I know John McGraw and other real veterans, especially in the National League, will accuse me of popping off on a subject I don't know a lot about. Well, it goes anyway! And as for Walter—I wasn't in the league when he was at his best. The old fastball that made him such a wizard ten years ago was a bit slower when I first looked it over. But Walter's reputation still lasted as I remembered it from my sandlot days.

I guess ballplayers talk more about pitching than any other single baseball subject. That's because base hits are the greatest joy in a ballplayer's life. In baseball we always figure that it's the base hits that bring a fellow his salary. Everett Scott used to comment on that a lot.

Scotty was never a very wicked hitter. And many times I've heard him grumbling about it. "The base hits you cut off don't mean anything in this league," Scotty used to say. "You can play your head off out there on the field, but it's the strong-backed .300 boys who get the money."

The first real discussion of Johnson I heard was on the train going to Washington in 1925, when I rejoined the club after being down in the minors. Johnson was due to pitch against us, and the boys were talking about his fastball.

Some of the younger fellows were talking about his speed. Babe and Scotty and Wallie Schang and some of the older chaps listened in.

Finally, Babe spoke up. "Say, you fellows never saw any swift at all." (Babe always refers to fastballs as the "swift.") "You should have seen that guy five years ago. You just see his arm swing, and then the ump yells 'Strike three.' Right when a guy would be hitting good, he comes into Washington and faces Walter. And socko! Five for a horse collar, and it would be a week before you'd get your eyes back in focus and hit your stride again." "Horse collar" is the baseball players' term for a zero in the hit column. In other words, five times at bat without a hit would be a horse collar, or a fat round zero.

To make a long story short, Walter pitched that afternoon. And I was literally scared to death when I stepped to the plate. The first pitch of Walter's was a fastball inside, and I guess I jumped back three feet. Muddy Ruel was catching.

"Stand up there, kid," Muddy said. "He won't kill you. Only break a bone or two."

Walter struck me out the first time—and I was the easiest strikeout he ever got. But the rest of the time, it was my day. I got two home runs and a triple off him and came back to the clubhouse at the end of the game half expecting the boys to give me a medal or a gold cup or something.

But they didn't. The only comment came from the Babe as we were in the showers.

"Pretty lucky for you that big bird wasn't right today," he said. "Watch out for him next time. He's apt to have his stuff."

I've faced Walter Johnson a lot since then. I've managed to get some hits, and I've struck out plenty. But I never met a finer fellow or knew a better sport than Walter. To my mind, he is just about the finest and cleanest character in baseball. I have never known him to have an argument with an umpire or another player. I have never heard him say an unkind thing or alibi a defeat.

A lot of people used to say baseball as a profession was a waste of time. All I can say to that is that any game which will produce a man like Walter Johnson after twenty years of competition is worthwhile. The Eddie Collinses, the Walter Johnsons, and men of that type are a credit to baseball. And they would be a credit to any other profession under the sun.

Sitting on the bench, even with a pennant-winning club, is a tiresome proposition. I know. I did it plenty.

As I look back on it now, I realize just how wise Miller Huggins was in keeping me there. I was about as green as any rookie who ever stepped into a uniform. The boys used to kid me about it a lot.

And a lot of times, they weren't kidding. I remember very well my first big league game. It was in 1923, toward the end of the season. Hug decided to start me at first base and told the fellows in the clubhouse. Joe Bush was slated to pitch that day, and it made him sore. He was having a good year and wanted to win that ball game.

"That kid don't know what it's all about," he complained to Huggins. "He'll pull some boner and lose the game for me."

The Babe kidded Joe back. "Let him have a chance, Bush," Babe said. "Maybe he'll sock one on the nose."

In the early part of the game, it looked as though Joe was right. We were playing Washington, a smart ball club. The score was 0 to 0 in the fourth, and Sam Rice was on third base, Bucky Harris was on first, and Joe Judge at bat. Joe put on the squeeze and laid a perfect bunt down between the pitcher's box and the first base line. I came in and fielded the ball all right, but I didn't know what to do with it. Rice was tearing for home, Harris was on his way to second, and Judge was coming toward first like a steam engine.

Maybe I was paralyzed, I don't know. Anyway, I just stood there while Rice scored and the other runners were safe.

I never saw Bush so sore.

"What's the matter, stupid?" he asked. "Got frozen brains? I suppose they teach you to think fast like that at Columbia!"

But the damage was done, and nothing could help me then. I just shut my mouth and went about my business. Later, I got a break. In the seventh inning, I came up with the bases full and smacked out a double that scored three runs and won the ball game.

I'll say this for Bush. He certainly was a good sport. At the end of the inning, he waited for me, and we walked across the diamond together. Joe put his arm around my shoulders and patted me on the back.

"I'll hand it to you, kid," he said. "You can certainly smack that apple. But what I said awhile ago still goes. You're so dumb it hurts. What you need to do is get out there and get wise to the game. You can't get by in this league on hitting alone."

It was pretty good advice, but I didn't pay much attention to it. Joe brought up the subject again. And he got me out on first base and bunted to me until I was blue in the face, teaching me how to cut off a run at the plate, how to hold the runner on first, and all the details of making a play that the day before had made me look like a sap.

I've heard a lot of stories about Joe Bush and his temper. And Joe was pretty quick to flare up when things went wrong. But behind all that was one of the best dispositions I ever knew. On the field and off, Joe was happy and carefree.

He loved to joke, and he kept everyone in good humor. He and Sam Jones roomed together for years, and I guess there was one of the greatest friendships in baseball. Both of them kidded me plenty—but they both taught me a lot too. When they left the Yankees, we all figured that we had lost two of the finest fellows who ever put on uniforms.

The chap who said that nothing was impossible in this world didn't know his baseball. There's two things that a fellow can't do, as I found out mighty early in my career.

You can't lick a cop, and you can't win an argument from an umpire. The first umpire I ever tried to win an argument from was Billy Evans, and I ran a poor second. It all happened in Cleveland in 1923. Ward was at bat and hit a ground ball down past [Walter] Lutzke that scored two runs. Billy called it foul.

I didn't think it was and told him so. I raved and ranted and waved my arms, and Billy just stood there and looked. Then, when I had finished, he turned to me.

"Well," he said, "are you all through?"

I said I was.

"Now that you've had your say," Billy continued, "you're out of the game. Beat it!"

I was sore, and I called Billy a lot of names and said a lot of things I shouldn't.

Billy listened without moving, and then without raising his voice or making a single gesture, he finished his sentence.

"That will cost you just $100," he said. "And don't forget this, young fellow. As long as you're in this league, the umpire's decision is official."

I was whipped. One hundred dollars was a lot of money, and I was a sick boy when I thought of it. But Benny Bengough saved me. Benny was standing by and heard Billy name the fine.

"Aw, you can't do that Billy," Benny said. "He's only getting $25 a week."

Billy grinned. "All right," he said, "just forget it, Lou. But chase yourself out of here and stay out. You're too excited to watch this ball game."

Yet there are a lot of people who say umpires aren't human.

I get a lot of laughs from the crowd when they get on the umpires. The fans over at the Stadium were riding Clarence Rowland one day. Finally, the Babe came to bat and after fouling two, he watched a third one go by.

Clarence called it a strike, and the Babe turned around quickly and said something. Then he gestured with his hands and stood there talking to Clarence. The fans were excited and started howling.

"Tell him a few things, Babe," they yelled. "He's a thief. Tell him about it!"

There was still an uproar when Babe walked back to the bench, and as he disappeared, one loud-voiced chap sitting alongside the dugout leaned half over the rail:

"I guess that will hold you, you big bum," he shouted at Rowland. "What he ought to do is smack you down."

The laugh of the whole thing is that Babe hadn't kicked at all. What he really said when he turned to Clarence was simply this:

"Holy mackerel, Clarence, did you see that one break? That fellow never has showed me a hook like that before. Where did he get that one?"

I've had plenty of arguments with umpires since then. But here's something for the fans to remember. In about ninety-five cases out of a hundred, the umpires call the close ones right. That's their business, and they get paid for it because they're good.

And here's another thing. Two-thirds of the time when the fans think players are arguing with umpires, they aren't really arguing at all.

Over in Washington one day, Huggins came rushing out of the bench at the end of a play to talk with the umpires. The fans booed and jeered and howled plenty. They thought he was kicking on a decision. What he really asked was about ground rules on a ball hit into the overflow crowd.

You get a lot of laughs from umpires. But so far as the players are concerned, most of the laughs are with them and not at them. It's the fans who provide the real fun.

Chapter 5

What sort of fellow is Ruth? What is Pennock like? And Meusel? And Lazzeri?

How do you like Speaker? And Cobb? And Johnson?

These are the sort of questions that every ballplayer hears. Fans, watching the games, know the stars as they appear on the field. But they all have the same curiosity as to the sort of chaps they are once they are out of their uniforms and put on the "civvies" of everyday life.

I don't know what the fans expect. Perhaps they want their baseball heroes to be different on the field and off. Perhaps they expect them to be eccentric and unusual. They're not. They're human, the same as everyone else. They have their homes and their families and their individual interests, the same as the doctor or the lawyer or the clerk.

A ball club, very naturally, is made up of men of varying types and varying personalities. On the Yankee ball club, for instance, there are men of nine different nationalities, drawn from seventeen different states. And they're thrown together because they have just one common interest—baseball.

On the field, they're all ballplayers. Off the field, they have a chance to practice the things which they like and enjoy most.

Most ballplayers have hobbies of some sort. Some of them are very interesting.

Herb Pennock, for instance, is an inveterate horseman. In the winter, Herb spends his time on his place at Kennett Square, Pennsylvania, looking after his horses and riding to hounds like a real English squire.

A lot of players are great hunters. Bob Shawkey is one of the best rifle shots in the game and spends two months out of every year hunting for big game in Canada. Veteran hunters tell me that Bob knows the Canadian woods better than many guides and can follow a trail tirelessly from morning to night. Eddie Collins and Tris Speaker are enthusiastic hunters, too, and are never so happy as when they're out in the woods with a gun on their shoulders.

Walter Johnson is a dog fancier, and at his home in Maryland, he has some of the finest hunting dogs in the country. Recently, when Walter celebrated his twentieth anniversary as a Washington pitcher, his friends and admirers showered him with gifts. But of all the things received, Walter valued most a little pup given him by Joe Engel, the Washington scout.

Twenty years ago, ballplayers were content to spend their off season in the corner saloon or at the neighborhood cigar store. Times have changed. Among ballplayers today are a lot of professional men who step from the diamond to their office. Muddy Ruel of the Washington Senators practices law. Eddie Farrell of the Boston Braves is a dentist. Garland Buckeye, the big Cleveland left hander, is a banker. Earle Combs, center fielder for the Yankees, taught school for several winters. Art Nehf, as everyone knows, is an electrical engineer and a very fine one.

It is a surprising thing how many ballplayers turn to golf for relaxation and amusement. And many of them are crack golfers too. "Jigger" Statz, Brooklyn outfielder, is one of the best golfers on the Pacific coast. Bob Shawkey is a wizard on the links, and Aaron Ward of the White Sox plays a round in the low eighties, as does Sam Rice of the Senators and Dazzy Vance of Brooklyn.

Moe Berg of the White Sox has one of the most interesting hobbies in baseball. Moe is a student, and for the past five or six years, he has spent the off season in school. He studied languages in the Sorbonne in Paris, studied law at Columbia, did special work at Princeton and Chicago. He is now one of the best educated men in baseball or out. Moe is living proof of the fact that an athlete can find interest in something other than outdoor activity. And thrive on it too.

When I went into big league baseball, I expected to be razzed and kicked about by the older players. In 1923, when I put on my first Yankee uniform, I half expected a fight or two before I had been there a week. As a college kid, I had heard stories of big league cliques and the feeling that always existed between the regulars and the rookies who were trying for their jobs.

That may have been true twenty years ago. I guess it was. When Ty Cobb broke in, he had to fight two-thirds of the players on the Detroit club before finally he won his spurs as a regular. But it's not true anymore.

I was kidded plenty, but it was all good-natured. Fellows like

Joe Bush and Sam Jones are natural born jokers. And I was a good subject for them. For there never was a greener rookie came to the league than me. I had lived all my life in New York, and I had never been away from the big town. Boston and Philadelphia and Washington were strange lands. Chicago and Philadelphia and St. Louis were foreign countries, as far as I was concerned.

One of the greatest laughs I ever gave the boys occurred in Chicago in 1923. We were sitting around the hotel lobby one evening "punching the bag" about this and that. I happened to be reading the sports page of one of the Chicago papers.

"Who pitched for the Cubs today?" Joe Dugan asked.

I looked at my paper. Across the top was a headline which said: "Cubs win; Bruins hold Pirates to one run."

"Why, I guess it was this guy Bruins," I said. "They only got one run off him." That started the boys off. And for two months, every time I came into the clubhouse, the gang had something to say about it. "How's Bruins today?" they'd ask. And "Well, do you think Bruins will lead the league this season?"

But it was all good-natured. And after a while, they forgot all about it and turned their attention to other things.

The point I started out to make was that breaking into the big leagues now is a lot simpler process than it used to be. Ballplayers today realize that their careers are limited. And they realize, too, that every promising rookie who comes along is a help rather than a hindrance.

In this connection, I never knew a finer fellow than Bob Shawkey. Bob is not only a smart fellow himself, but he has the ability to teach others. And he's always willing to do it. George

Pipgras is one of Bob's pupils. When George first joined the club back in 1923, Bob started working with him, and he has helped a lot.

If that happened ten or fifteen years ago, instead of being helped by the veterans, George would have had to fight all his own battles without a word of encouragement or aid from the old timers.

We had a great gang of rookies in that first training camp in New Orleans. Pipgras was there and Mike Gazella, both of them with the Yankees now. Gink Hendrick, now Brooklyn's best batter, was in camp. So was Hinkey Haines, now one of the best professional football players. The boys are still talking about them.

"The freshest and dumbest lot of rookie ballplayers I ever saw," the Babe said the other day. "The fact that most of them are still playing in the league is the tipoff on the sort of baseball that's played nowadays."

I have been around the big leagues now for the best part of five seasons. I have seen most of the modern star players in action, and I have talked with them on the field and off.

And the biggest hearted, the most whole-souled chap of the lot is Babe of the Yanks.

A lot of unkind things have been written about the Babe. He is no plaster saint, and he admits it. He has made mistakes during his career, and he knows that. But through it all, he stands out as the greatest of the great in baseball; a wonderful all around ballplayer and a corking fine fellow.

Some people claim the Babe is a poser. He isn't at all. Others say he is insincere. He isn't that. I've watched him through all those seasons. In those rookie days when I needed friends, his "H'ye, kid" was the most cheering greeting I knew. I admired him then as a player. Now that I've been around and come to know him better, I admire him as a man as well.

There never has been a player more generous of his time and money; there never has been a figure in baseball with more personality; and I never have known a man of more rare good humor or such kindliness—providing you don't try to rough him up or take advantage.

There's an old saying that any man who is loved by kids and dogs is one hundred per cent. The Babe qualifies on both counts. Some people think that the affection he shows for kids is a pose. It isn't at all. Children can impose on him any time and get away with it. I've seen him stand outside the clubhouse for forty minutes at a time signing programs and baseballs and autograph books for youngsters.

Up at Toronto in an exhibition game a couple of years ago, the kids mobbed the field as the game ended. There must have been a thousand of them, and they all made a bee line for Babe. They struck him like a huge wave, and he went down flat on his face, literally buried under a landslide of kids.

It looked as though he must be trampled to death, and players and cops formed a flying wedge to rescue him. But before we got there, he emerged smiling, two or three youngsters clinging to his broad back, others hanging on his legs, and one under each arm. Most players would have been angered and disgusted. But the Babe was smiling as he trotted to the runway and still smiling when he disappeared under the stands.

As he started down in the dugout, he happened to look back. One little youngster was still standing over by first base, crying. Babe turned back thru the mob again and went to the kid.

"What's the matter, kid?" he asked.

"I got my hand stepped on," the little fellow whimpered. "It hurts."

"That's all right," Babe replied, taking the lad in his arms. "We'll get that fixed." And back he ploughed through the mob, the youngster held in his arms.

"Look out, here comes the ambulance!" he called. Then he took the lad into the clubhouse, and Babe bandaged the sore finger himself. After that, he gave the lad a baseball, a pat on the back, and sent him away smiling. That's typical of the Babe.

To the public, he is "Babe," but to the players he's always "Jedge." It's a name Benny Bengough gave him a few seasons ago, and it has stuck—just the Yankees' own pet name for the greatest player in the game.

There'll never be another like him—never again a man with the same ability, the same good humor and frankness; never another so likeable and so good-natured. If I mention him unduly in these stories, it is only because he occupies so large a place in my baseball experience; if I give him loads of credit, it is no more than he deserves. There are other great ballplayers—and then there's "Jedge"—standing alone and without a rival.

I suppose every big league ballplayer gets discouraged now and then.

I did. And one day I came close to quitting the game entirely. It was in 1925, the year the Yankees were kicking around at the bottom of the league, taking it on the chin from everybody.

I had slid around that bench for so long that I had worn out two sets of uniform trousers, and apparently there wasn't a chance for me to break into the lineup. Finally, in Chicago, word came to us that Manager Huggins was going up to St. Paul to look over a new shortstop.

That night, I went up to Hug's room.

He was packing his bag for the trip, and when I came in, he just looked up for a moment, said, "Hello, Lou," and went on with his packing. I didn't know what to say—I stammered and stuttered a bit, and finally blurted out:

"Say, Hug, try and get me a job in St. Paul, will you? I'm tired of sitting on the bench, and I want to play ball every day."

Right there, Miller Huggins proved to me that he was a real fellow and a mighty smart man. Some managers, having a rookie bust in on them like that probably would have cursed a bit and chased him out of the room. But not Hug.

"Sit down, Lou," he said.

And then he told me a few things.

"Listen, Lou," he said, "I'd like to send you out of the league, but I can't get waivers on you. I know how you feel. I went through the same thing when I was a kid breaking in, and it's mighty discouraging. Now, I'm going to tell you something. You've got a good chance to make the big league grade. But you're not good enough yet. You're too green, and you've got too many things to learn. Some things I can teach you. A lot of things you'll have to learn for yourself, and you'll have to learn them right out there on the bench.

"You think you can play better than some of the fellows I'm using out there every day. I know you can't. Those fellows will know their business, they're smart, and they've learned a lot of things you never heard of. I believe eventually you'll make the grade. But you're not ready yet. Now, just go back there and keep your mouth shut and your eyes and ears open. When the time comes, you'll get your chance. Remember that a real ballplayer is the guy who can keep his head up when the going is rough, and who is so anxious to play ball that he would spend ten years on the bench, if necessary, for a chance to break into the lineup."

Reduced to writing, that little talk doesn't sound so important. But to a discouraged rookie, it was the greatest thing that ever happened. I went back downstairs with a grin, determined to stick it out. And I did.

About a month later, when we were back to the Stadium one day, Hug called me into his office alongside the dressing rooms.

"You're playing today, Lou," he said. "I'm putting you in regularly. Don't be worried if you boot one, and don't get excited. Just do the best you can."

That afternoon, Benny Bengough, Howard Shanks, Ernie Johnson, and myself all broke into the Yankee lineup.

After three years of waiting, my dream had come true. I was a regular big league ballplayer at last.

Stepping from the college campus to the big league diamond may be thrilling and all that, but it's tough too.

The baseball we played at Columbia was kindergarten stuff

to the big league brand, and I found it out about two hours after I put on a Yankee uniform. That was three years ago, and I'm still taking lessons.

The biggest difference of all is in the pitching.

Don't misunderstand me. The big league pitchers' curveball doesn't break any further and their fast one isn't much faster than a lot of the curves and fast ones I looked over in college. I don't know of any pitcher in the big leagues, for instance, who had more real "stuff" than Owen Carroll had when he was a college pitcher playing for Holy Cross.

But here's the difference. College pitchers pitch with their arms. The boys in the big leagues pitch with their heads. Ask Owen Carroll. He found it out two years ago when he came from Holy Cross to the Tigers. Owen was knocked loose from his ears every time he started. He found out that he couldn't stand up there and throw that fast one past the hitters. And the break on his curves didn't bother anyone, either, for they knew when it was coming.

Big league pitchers study their business. Take Bob Shawkey, for instance. Bob has got every hitter in the American League catalogued. He can tell what they hit best and what gives them trouble. They go even further than that. They even watch to see where a certain hitter will hit a certain pitch. One hitter may hit a low ball outside to left. Some other hitter will hit the same ball to right. Shawkey knows all those things—and whenever a new man comes into the league, Bob gets busy right away to get the dope on him.

That's why Bob is so valuable to the Yankees. He coaches the young pitchers and tells them all the things he has found out in the 15 years he has worn a big league uniform.

Urban Shocker is one of the cagiest pitchers I know. Urb hasn't a lot of stuff anymore. But he has a head and uses it. When you're up there hitting against Urb, you can mark it down that you won't get a good one to hit at. He plays the corners and never puts one down the "alley."

The fact that a pitcher has a lot of stuff doesn't mean that he'll make a great pitcher. Walter Beall, who used to be with the Yankees, had more natural stuff than any man I ever saw on the mound. But he didn't know what to do with it. George Pipgras three years ago had as much as any man on the club. But it took George two years in the minors before he learned how to pitch so he could get by.

You can sit down right now and make a list of the best pitchers in the two leagues—and then you can copy the same list for the smartest pitchers. Jesse Haines and [William] Sherdel of the Cardinals; Pennock and Hoyt of the Yankees; Burleigh Grimes and [Lawrence] Benton of the Giants; Lee Meadows of the Pirates; [Harold] Carlson of the Cubs; Shocker and [Walter "Dutch"] Ruether of the Yankees; Jess Petty of the Brooklyn Dodgers; George Uhle of Cleveland; Jack Quinn of the Athletics; smart as foxes, all of them. And tough! Boy, when they come any tougher than these fellows, it'll be time for me to move on to some other league where they toss 'em up without thinking.

And the funny part of it is that when you're up there hitting against fellows like that, they don't seem to have a thing. You swing, and swing and swing and strike out or pop up and go back to the bench feeling like a sap.

The first day I joined the Yankees, I saw batters go up and take their cut, then come back to the bench saying, "He hasn't got a thing." They're still doing it—and always will.

But it's the fellows who "haven't got a thing" who are pitching the best ball. They know their business. They pitch with their heads.

Chapter 6

There are two kinds of ballplayers. One is the fan's ballplayer. The other is the ballplayer's ballplayer. Fellows like the Babe, Ty Cobb, or Frankie Frisch qualify in both classes. They have the color and the pepper that appeals to the fans, and at the same time, they have the real baseball ability that appeals to players as well.

Chaps like Harry Heilmann, Muddy Ruel, Earle Combs, Bob Meusel, Ross Youngs, and fellows of that type are ballplayer's ballplayers. They don't make such a hit with the crowd, but other players recognize them as real stars.

They're what we call "money ballplayers." That means they're at their best in the pinches, when the whole game or maybe a pennant depends on a single play.

My first introduction to a real illustration of "money ballplaying" came during the 1923 World Series. I was sitting on the bench through all those games, and I was nervous as anything. Finally, we came down to the final game. A lot of fans will remember that one. It was at the Polo Grounds, and Art Nehf, one of the finest little sportsmen who ever wore spiked shoes, was going great guns for the Giants.

We simply couldn't touch him, and it looked like a sure

Giant victory. But in the eighth, Art weakened. His control went "blooey," and the Yankee rally started. Art was taken out, and Rosy Ryan came in to strike out the Babe for the second out.

Everyone on the bench was half crazy except Bob Meusel. He was as cool and calm as though he was taking hitting practice.

Bob was next up, and we needed a hit to win. If Bob couldn't come through, we were sunk.

"Watch that curveball," Hug told him. "He'll curve you every pitch. Watch it, Bob, watch it!"

Hug was excited too and made no effort to conceal it.

Bob strolled over to the water tank and took a long drink.

"If he curves one to me, I'll knock it down his throat," he said quietly. Then he pointed out between shortstop and second base. "See that hole there?" he said. "Well, watch your World Series go right down through there."

The rest is history. Bob singled for the sweetest single I ever saw—and right between short and second. Two runners scored. A moment later, Bob came back to the dugout. Everyone rushed up to congratulate him. It looked like a mob scene. Bob only grinned and took a drink.

"He curved it, and I socked it," he said.

That's what you call a money ballplayer. Bob Meusel is one of the greatest ones I know. Frankie Frisch is another great money player. Frankie has pulled plays in a World Series that seemed almost impossible. Rogers Hornsby is another of that type. Rog is dangerous any time, but in the pinches when the game depends on him, he's twice as dangerous as he is any other time.

The fan's ballplayer is the fellow who packs them in at the

gate, but it's the ballplayer's ballplayer who rises to meet emergencies and comes through in the pinches. Fellows like George Burns never got many hands from the fans—but among the ballplayers, they rate aces high.

Of course, it's great to be both. But if I can't have the attributes that make me qualify both ways, then I'll prefer to be the ballplayer's ballplayer every time. Cheers sound pleasantly in a fellow's ear always, but there's a lot more kick in knowing that you're doing your job well even if the cheers don't echo so loudly.

When I first came to the Yankees in 1923, the thing that astonished me most was the tremendous amount of "fan mail" which was delivered to the Babe every day. "Doc" Woods, Yankee trainer, acted as a sort of secretary to the Babe and used to bring the letters in by the basket full. To read all those letters and try to answer them would be impossible. Babe used to pass them around the clubhouse to the various players.

"Look 'em over," he'd say. "If they are all right, let me have 'em back."

So we'd act as a sort of committee, going over all those letters. Most of them were from kids, and usually they wanted some favor. A ball, perhaps, or a glove, or a bat, or an autograph.

Babe always had one set rule, and he still has it.

If the letter was from some unfortunate, some cripple or orphan or kid who was up against it, it had to be answered.

He got one, one day from a little kid in Germany. It was written in German, and Babe gave it to me to translate.

"I'm just a poor little boy but I've been following all you do in the papers," the kid wrote, "and someday I hope I can grow up and become a great athlete like you. I'm writing just to wish you luck and let you know that I'm pulling for you every day."

"Don't he want something?" the Babe asked. "Doesn't he ask for a ball or something?"

"Not a thing," I told him.

"Well, I'm a son of a gun," Babe retorted. "Just wishes me luck, eh?"

He turned to Woodie.

"Hey, Woodie, get me a ball and a glove," he ordered, "and a good strong box. I'm going to send 'em to that kid in Germany."

And he did, too—along with a nice letter which I put into German for him.

The Babe is like that. And people who say he is high hat or upstage are crazy. He's just a big kid—with a heart as big as his own shoulders.

I'll never forget a bit of advice the Babe gave me when I first joined the club. "Listen, kid," he said. "You're a good hitter and a hard hitter. Take your cut when you go up there to the plate, but don't let anyone get you in the habit of trying to park that ball out of the lot on every swing. I have to do it, for that's what I'm paid for. But it's bad business.

"I wish I could go up there at the plate like Joey Sewell and stand flat footed and take the sort of swing he does," the Babe added. "Why, I'd bat .500 in this league. And so can you if you'll watch yourself. If you just take an ordinary swing, you'll get plenty of home runs—and you'll get a lot bigger hitting average too. That's what counts in this business."

Babe meant it too. He likes to hit home runs—but he's tickled to death when he gets a chance to lay one down occasionally. Despite all his home run hitting, I honestly believe the Babe would rather fool an infielder by laying one down and beating it out. I've seen him chuckle all through a game because he was able to do just that thing.

"Did you see me fool him that time?" he'd say when he came back to the bench. "Boy, I guess Willie Keeler never bunted a better one than that one."

I've had a lot of good advice since I've been in baseball.

The old idea about ballplayers not being willing to help each other is not so. George Sisler was one of the first men in the league to show me how to shift my feet in covering first. When I came into the league, that was one of my many weaknesses, and George was one of the stars of the game. There was no reason why he should take any interest in a mere rookie. But he did. And not only once but a score of times.

Ty Cobb has taken many minutes of his time showing me how to slide and how to run bases. I never got to be very good. I guess I'm a poor student. But that isn't Ty's fault. He was willing enough to be my teacher. Ernie Johnson, Bob Shawkey, Sam Jones, and Wallie Schang all went out of their way to help me when I broke in. And one of the finest things that ever happened to me came from Wallie Pipp. I had just taken Wallie's job at first. A lot of fellows would have been sore and hurt about that. But not Wallie. I hadn't been playing a week when he came to me.

"Lou," he said, "you've got the makings of a good first baseman. But you've got a lot to learn. There's a lot about the job I don't know. But I've been around a long time. I'm about through.

But I'd like to show you a few of the tricks I know, if it won't make you sore."

You can't beat that sort of spirit, anywhere. I guess maybe that's the answer to the howlers who are always saying that baseball players are roughnecks and ingrates and ne'er do wells. I don't think there's any man in any profession who would do a finer thing than Wallie Pipp did for me.

But the best advice I ever had in my life came from the Babe— and only a few weeks ago.

We were sitting on the bench one day during hitting practice. Babe was clowning with some of the opposing players, and they were kidding him about the money he had made and lost. When they left, he slid over on the bench where I was. And he wasn't smiling, either.

"I've been pretty much of a sap in my day," he said. "I've played around a lot, and I've wasted a lot of money that I ought to have saved. But I've learned something. I'm getting wise to myself at last. Let me give you a tip, Lou. The best advice that I can give you or anyone else can give you is just this: 'Save your money.'"

The Babe is something of a philosopher in his way, and he was philosophic that day.

"Don't mind the cheers," he said. "They don't mean anything. In this business we're in, you hear cheers one day and jeers the next. You're a good fellow as long as you're playing a great game, but the minute you slip, they forget all about your good plays. But there's one thing they can't take away from you. That's the money you save, and if you're as smart as I think you are, you'll start in salting it away right now. Get your pile while it comes easy.

Someday the going will be tough, and then you'll be sorry if you haven't saved what you should. Just take a tip from me. I know."

And he does.

Babe has got wise to himself the last few years. He's finally saving his money, and if he stays in baseball a few more years, he'll be able to step out and be independent. And that's what he wants everyone else to do—and says so.

As I said before, that's the best advice I've ever had since I've been playing baseball. I don't believe in being a tightwad or a miser or anything like that. But baseball is a profession, and it's up to me and all the rest of us to make the most of our profession while we can.

You have noticed that in all these stories I have said little or nothing about Miller Huggins.

I've been waiting until the end of my story to write of the man whom I consider the shrewdest, best, and smartest manager in baseball.

Hug is a peculiar little chap. He's shy and bashful. He hates the limelight, and he's always willing to see the other fellow grab all the glory. But he's one hundred per cent as a manager.

There have been stories printed from time to time about dissension on the Yankee club. Rumors have gone out that Huggins can't get along with his players and that there is strife in the ranks. That's bunk. Pure and simple bunk. There isn't a man on the whole Yankee club right now who doesn't regard Hug as the best in the country—and that goes for fellows on other clubs as well.

I'll say this for Hug. He's the most patient manager I ever knew. When I broke in, I was green and awkward and half afraid. I made boot after boot, and bad play after bad play. A lot of fellows would have cussed me out and tossed me out of the lineup. But not Hug. He stuck with me and encouraged me and helped me.

"You do the best you can, and I'll stay with you," was his motto.

And it wasn't for me alone. He has played the same sort of game with Tony Lazzeri and Mark Koenig, and every other young fellow who has broken into the lineup. I don't believe there ever was a squarer man or one who knew the inside of baseball more thoroughly.

Hug has had a pretty tough time. I can remember when most of the newspaper boys were riding him and panning him and making fun of him. But he never said a word. Just kept sawing wood. And he has made his worst critics like it.

Hug came to the Yankees ten years ago. Since that time, he has won five pennants and has finished in the money every year but one. In 1925 he tore his old club completely apart and started to rebuild. Some folks said he was crazy, but he followed his own judgment. In one year, he built up a new club that was good enough to go out and win a pennant.

That's the tip-off on Hug.

Just a great little fellow, as loyal to his ballplayers as a mother is to her children. He never boasts, and he isn't given to bag punching like a lot of fellows. He never pushes himself forward, and he's more than willing to sit back and let the other fellow get the credit. But he knows his baseball—and he is the best teacher I ever had the privilege of being with.

A lot of people say Huggins lacks inspiration; they say he is a poor leader, but take this from me: There isn't a man on the Yankee club who wouldn't fight for Miller Huggins. Maybe at one time, some of them have doubted his judgment and ability, but he has proved himself to them. They don't doubt him any longer.

They're for him, and that goes for everyone on the club, from the Babe right down to the newest rookie. As for the younger fellows like myself, we owe him a lot that we can't repay. No manager in the world could have been more kindly or more considerate or more patient than Miller Huggins, and we know it.

Perhaps I might have made the grade on some other club. There may be other managers who would have treated me as squarely or taught me as much baseball. But I doubt it. I've watched 'em all, and I've studied their methods and their ways. I'm convinced that Miller Huggins is the class of the bunch.

A few seasons of big league baseball are enough to convince the players that baseball—like law or medicine—is a profession.

It doesn't take the cheers of the fans to tell a man when he has made a good play, nor are the jeers necessary to let him know when he has pulled a "boner." Occasionally you hear some cold-blooded expert express the opinion that players are nonchalant. That they don't care how they go, so long as the pay check arrives regularly.

I haven't been around long—but I've been up in the majors long enough to know that that is all wrong. I've seen a player come back to the bench in tears because he "booted" one in a crisis. I've seen men on the bench jump to their feet and shout like school kids over some particularly good play.

People say ballplayers are selfish—but I've seen them heap congratulations on other men, as college kids congratulate their own heroes.

It's the spirit of sport—and it's just as prevalent among professional ballplayers as it was on the college field at Columbia. You can't kill the spirit to win—whether a man plays for mere amusement or finds in play a means of earning an honest livelihood. The cheers and the jeers are all part of the game. We learn to take them as they come without undue thrill or undue malice. But every big league ballplayer has some real friend whose advice he values and whose opinion means more than that of all the world put together.

I have one true friend like that—my mother.

Since I was a kid playing on the sandlots, my mother has been the first to encourage me in my efforts. Through my college career and on through my first seasons with the Yankees, she was always ready with a kindly word of encouragement. She didn't want me to go into professional baseball. She wanted me to finish college instead.

But when I did sign a contract, she immediately forgot her own desires and became my most loyal booster. She's up at the Yankee Stadium almost every day the Yankees are home. And the Yankee ball club is now her ball club. They are all her boys—

and no one in the whole world is happier when we win, or has more sympathy when we lose.

I have many friends who have been nice to me; friends who have shown me real favors and whose friendship I value beyond expression. But from first to last, it has been my mother who has encouraged me and aided me most. I don't say these things to be sentimental. Every man, I suppose, owes to his own mother the same debt of gratitude.

My first appearance in a big league uniform brought a thrill. But I think it meant even more to my mother than it did to me. My first World Series was the same. And when, during the World Series, I crashed out a hit that scored the winning run and turned to see my mother smiling through her tears, I appreciated then just how much her life was wrapped up in me and mine in hers.

I'm still young at this baseball game. With any sort of break, I hope to continue playing for many years. But if I live to rival the record of Cobb; if I should succeed in breaking all the records in the book, I would still feel that my mother deserved most of the credit.

For hers was the first encouragement I ever had; her loyalty has endured where all others have failed—she is now, and will always be, the greatest pal I ever had.

Chapter 7

The so-called "home run derby" of 1927 is over.

The winner is Babe Ruth. And no one is happier than myself. During the season, the newspapers have been more than kind to me. They have compared me to the Babe; they have called me the "new home run king"; they have given me the kindliest sort of criticism.

For which I am grateful—but—and this is honest—I never expected to beat the Babe in honors, and I never expected to break that 1921 record. After all is said and done, there is just one Babe. He stands alone and incomparable. He is the greatest slugger of all time, and in my humble opinion, there will never be another like him.

Unless he breaks it himself, I believe that 1921 record of fifty-nine home runs in a season will stand forever. I hope it does.

I owe much to the Babe. He has advised me and taught me and helped me more than I can tell. At times during the season, when I was leading him in home runs, the opinion prevailed that there was a feud between Babe and myself. Nothing could be further from the truth. When I would hit one, Babe would be the first to congratulate me.

In private and in public, he has always been my best booster.

And I really believe he is as delighted when I succeed in breaking a record or establishing a new mark as I am myself. There is nothing small, nothing selfish about the Babe.

And now a word about home run hitting. If the ball goes in the bleachers, well and good. If it goes for a single that scores a run, better still. I am proud of my record for driving in runs. I think I have a right to be. And if I live to be ninety and play baseball every day of that time, I will still get a thrill when I pound out a hit that sends a run over the plate.

But I am not a rival of the Babe. To consider myself one would be presumptuous. There is only one Babe Ruth, and never before has there been a player who could hit a ball as far or as frequently. He stands alone.

And don't forget this.

Babe Ruth is something else besides a home run hitter. He is a great ballplayer. Babe would rather see the Yankees win a ball game than to hit five home runs and lose. If a situation arises which demands a sacrifice, the Babe will do it willingly and gladly. Many times I've seen him go up there and shorten his stride and cut his swing in a frank effort to hit the ball just over the infield. I've seen him take strikes right through the middle, in order that a steal might be put over or a play made that would help win the ball game.

Does that sound like he was out for home runs, without regard to team welfare or team play?

Not by a long shot, it doesn't. And he isn't.

He hits home runs because he is a great hitter. When he gets hold of one, it just naturally sails out of the park.

Some folks think the Babe can do nothing else but hit. That's a laugh. He's a great ballplayer in every sense. He can throw, he can run, he can field. There is no smarter player in the game—no player with keener baseball instinct or better baseball judgment.

To talk of me, or anyone else, rivaling the Babe is to laugh.

All I hope to do is just the best I can. If I have a good year and hit a lot of homers, I'm happy. But if I don't, it's quite all right.

So far as I am concerned, the Babe's record is safe. He is the greatest of the great—and I honestly believe that the only man who ever has a chance of breaking his record is Babe Ruth himself.*

---

* Gehrig wrote this before the season ended. Ruth hit two homers on September 29 and his final four-bagger—number sixty, which broke his own 1921 record—the following day.

Chapter 8

— The 1927 World Series —

Preview

I guess if I live to play in twenty World Series, I would still get a tremendous kick out of them. There is something about the crowds, and the push and the jam and the excitement that gets into a fellow's blood.

It isn't nervousness so much as it is just sheer joy at being in the swim and the thrill of knowing that you're a member of a team good enough to be fighting it out for the world championship. Old timers like the Babe and Bob Meusel and Herbie Pennock don't feel that way, I guess. It's an old story to them. But to me it's still new and interesting, and it gives me a great kick. I admit it.

And here's the funny part. The biggest thrill comes before the games actually start. I learned that last year, and I imagine this Series will be about the same. For two days before the Series opened, I was like a kid starting in at a new school. I was half jubilant and half afraid. But once we put on uniforms and took the field, once the first ball was pitched and the first throw made, then it was just another ball game.

I guess most young players are that way. For me to try and

dope out the Series would be nonsense. I'm a mere kid at this baseball business. It's up to me to sit back and keep quiet. I've never been in the National League, and I've been in the American League just long enough to learn what it's all about.

If there's any real doping to be done, I'll leave that to Manager Huggins and some of the old timers. My business, as I see it, is to do what I'm told and say nothing. But naturally, I have some impressions. I believe the Yankees will win.

Naturally. And I know this. We've got a good ball club; a better club than a lot of people think. Some of the experts have figured that the Yankees would crack, since they have so many young players. I'm one of the young players. I know how a young player feels. And I don't believe we'll crack.

We may lose, of course, but if we do, it will be because we were honestly beaten and not because we broke down. And I don't look for the Pirates to crack, either. They've been through a hard, hard campaign. They came from behind to win, and when a team can do that, they're not the sort who break wide open from World Series excitement.

When we came into Pittsburgh yesterday, the papers were full of stories about how the Pirates would stop the Yankees if they stopped Ruth and myself. That's complimentary, but it's a laugh. Here's a tip for Pirate pitchers.

If they go into this Series figuring that Ruth and I are the only men they have to look out for, they're apt to find themselves knocked right loose from the ball park. Meusel, Combs, Lazzeri, Koenig, Dugan, and the rest are just as dangerous as the Babe and myself.

And the minute any opposing pitcher starts to let down when he's pitching to those chaps, he's flirting with destruction. Twenty-four hours from now, we'll have a line on what the Series holds. Not that the first game means victory one way or the other; it doesn't. But it does give a line on the system of play of the two clubs, and it gives a little dope on comparative ability.

The Yankees have had a look at the Pirate playing field. Most of us had never seen it before, and we were a lot interested. Now for the benefit of those fans who are wondering what our sluggers will do on Forbes Field. The field isn't a lot different from the Stadium. Right field is just as easy a target here as it is in New York. The left field stands are considerably further away. But that's to our advantage. The Yankees, for the most part, get their long, hard hits to right. Forbes Field is ideal in that respect.

Manager Huggins last night called us all together—our last meeting before the Series starts. Maybe you're interested in what he said. Hug wasted no time worrying about the Pirates or what they might do. He may have discussed hitting weaknesses with the pitchers. I don't know about that. But in talking to the club, he stressed just one point.

"Just remember that this Series is just another ball game," Huggins said. "All I ask is that you fellows go out there and play the same sort of ball that you've played all season. I don't want you to think you've got to do the unusual. You don't. Just play your normal game."

And that was about the extent of Hug's instructions.

A lot of fellows tell us that [Remy] Kremer is the best pitcher in the National League, and they pick him to give us more trouble than anyone else on the Pirate staff. But if Hoyt is right, and I think he will be, we don't need to worry. Waite can pitch against the best there is—and win. He proved it during the season.

The Yankees have never faced such pitching as they will see in this Series, some of the critics say. The Pittsburgh pitchers have never pitched against as hard-hitting a club as the Yankees, either. The rule works both ways.

But the next twenty-four hours will tell more about what is going to happen. I hope we win the first game. I believe we will. But whether we win or we lose, I'm still confident that the Yankees will grab off the Series. For I'm frank in believing that the 1927 Yankees are one of the best ball clubs of all times.

Game 1

Yankees 5, Pirates 4

The first round is over, and the Yankees are in front. I put it that way because that is the way I thought of it as we went through those first nine innings—as a fight in which each boxer was over anxious and, here and there, suffered because of it. We won because we made fewer mistakes and because we got the jump almost as soon as the game began and kept hustling.

The main reasons for our victory, other than the jump we got and our aggressiveness, were the fine hitting and fielding of Babe Ruth, the great work of Tony Lazzeri and Mark Koenig, a couple of Pacific coast boys, around second base, and the splendid relief pitching of Wilcy Moore. The Pirates drawing the finish very fine, always were dangerous, but they couldn't get by the obstacles set up by Ruth, Lazzeri, Koenig, and Moore.

Waite Hoyt, probably the best right-handed pitcher in either league this year, just wasn't himself. He had the Pirate batters pegged right and didn't make any mistakes in that respect, but his control was a little off, and, of course, he got into jams that ordinarily he would have avoided easily. It's hard to say what it is that takes the edge off a pitcher's control. It may be a number of things. In this instance, since Hoyt had so much stuff, I am inclined to think he was just trying a little too hard. In his next shot at the Pirates, which will come when both clubs have settled down and the Series is more of a work-a-day affair, I am sure he will have little trouble winning as handily as he did in a majority of his games during the championship season.

Ruth was great. I knew he would be—and I don't claim to be an expert on the strength of that, either. Anyone who saw him go smacking his way up to the end of the American League season, hitting the tar out of the ball almost every time he stepped to the plate, knew that he was right and that the Series would find him in the same form. He simply didn't give the Pirate pitchers a chance to set themselves; in three of his four times at bat, he hit the first ball, and the other time he hit the second ball. There isn't much chance for a pitcher to work on a batter who crashes the first ball for a base hit.

Another fine contribution that Babe made to the game was his catch of [Harold "Pie"] Traynor's fly in the first inning. With one run in, two out, and Paul Waner on third base, he went almost to the foul line for that one. Had it got away from him, the

Pirates would have gone into the lead and might not have been easy to catch, but Babe stopped them short. This brings to mind once more that Ruth, usually regarded only as a wonderful hitter, is a wonderful fielder as well and just as useful to our club in the field as he is at the plate.

Wilcy Moore, one of the most remarkable relief pitchers in baseball, was just as effective in this game as he was on so many occasions during the championship season. The fact that he was pitching for the first time in a World Series game and facing a club he never had seen before didn't seem to bother him in the least. He had his old sinker ball working to perfection, and, under the circumstances, the Pirates didn't have a chance to beat him any more than any other club you can think of would have had under the same circumstances.

The Pirates are a splendid club, even if I do think we will beat them in the Series just as we beat them yesterday—by hustling all the time and coming through with a lot of stuff whenever we needed it.

I never had seen the Waner brothers before, but I am prepared to believe all I ever heard about them. They're a couple of fine ballplayers. Our big trick is to keep them off the bases. It will not be easy, I'll admit, but I think we can do it or at least keep them from getting around if they do get on.

Ray Kremer must be a good pitcher. I could tell that, even if he wasn't himself in this game any more than Hoyt was. Like Hoyt, he was over anxious. He was trying to keep the high ball for us, and when his control wavered, he was aiming at the plate and making the balls too good.

1

Young Lou Gehrig would not learn English until he entered Public School 132 at the age of five. As a German-speaking child, his studies and social life suffered. The only surviving child of four, Lou became sensitive and shy, traits that would trouble him his entire life.

2

A proud graduate of PS 132. Although an enthusiastic ballplayer, Lou could not hit and was afraid to catch a ball. Swimming was a saving grace and allowed for social interaction with kids his own age.

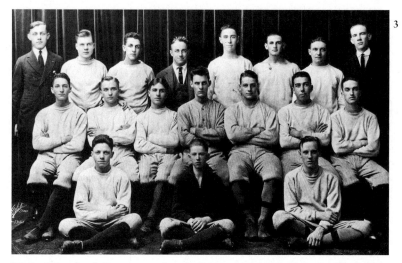

High School of Commerce baseball team in 1920. Lou is third from the right in the middle row. His grand slam in the ninth inning against Chicago's best high school team led to his photograph appearing in the New York newspapers.

4

Lou attended Columbia University on a football scholarship, where he competed as running back, tackle, and punter. He played every position with the zeal of a bulldozer in high gear.

5

After the football season, Lou began practice for the Columbia baseball team where he starred as a pitcher and first baseman. He set records as a member of the Lions ball club.

Yankees scout Paul Krichell signed Lou after seeing how hard he could smack a baseball. Here is Lou on June 11, 1923, his first day as a Yankee. After hitting some screaming line drives during batting practice, veteran players agreed that young Gehrig might have a future in the majors.

Lou was a Yankee only five weeks before being sent to the minors under the tutelage of Pat O'Connor, manager of the Hartford Senators. He needed to work through his defects by playing every day rather than sitting on the bench.

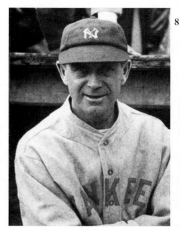

Lou was sent back to the Yankees where he began to thrive. He was devastated by the sudden death of legendary Yankees manager Miller Huggins in 1929, saying that Huggins's death "as far as baseball is concerned is nothing short of a national calamity."

Lou's mother, Christina, doted on her son and rarely missed a home game. She even accompanied Lou to spring training, where she could look after her little boy. His father, Heinrich, attended as many home games as he could, but he was often unable to leave a job to see afternoon contests.

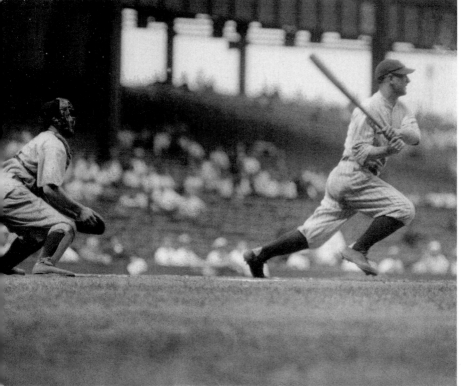

Opposing pitchers feared this swing that sent line drives into the right field bleachers during critical situations. While Babe Ruth hit high flies for home runs, Lou drove the ball on a direct line so that it was still gaining elevation when it hit the bleachers.

Lou during his breakout season of 1927, the same year *Following the Babe* was published. His spectacular hitting resulted in his being named Most Valuable Player in the American League.

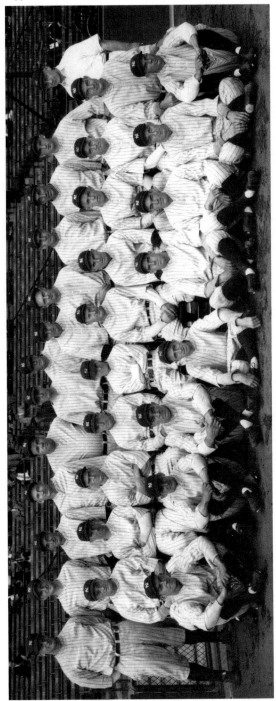

The 1927 New York Yankees. Popularly known as Murderers' Row, this team sent its manager and six players to the National Baseball Hall of Fame. From left to right, back row: Lou Gehrig (1B), Herb Pennock (P), Tony Lazzeri (2B), Wilcy Moore (P), Babe Ruth (RF), Don Miller (BP pitcher), Bob Meusel (LF), Bob Shawkey (P), Waite Hoyt (P), Joe Giard (P), Ben Paschal (OF), Joe Styborski (P), Al "Doc" Woods (trainer). Middle row: Urban Shocker (P), Joe Dugan (3B), Earle Combs (CF), Charley O'Leary (coach), Miller Huggins (manager), Art Fletcher (coach), Mark Koenig (SS), Dutch Ruether (P), John Grabowski (C), George Pipgras (P). Front row: Julian Wera (3B), Mike Gazella (UI), Pat Collins (C), Eddie Bennett (mascot), Benny Bengough (C), Ray Morehart (2B), Myles Thomas (P), Cedric Durst (OF).

Lou and Babe Ruth. These home run hitters knew how to clown around. This duo's hitting power was so inseparable in the lineup, Ruth third and Gehrig cleanup, that the players were given the numbers 3 and 4 when the Yankees first put numbers on uniforms in 1929.

14

Lou displayed the muscles that gave him his power at the plate. A lifelong believer in physical fitness, he never tired of exercising or playing baseball.

The *Oakland Tribune* used this photograph of Lou and his mom to announce his "Following the Babe" columns. This image perfectly encapsulates the close relationship between Lou and Christina until his marriage to Eleanor.

Lou liked to relax at Lake Oscawana, where his agent, Christy Walsh, owned a cottage. Located an hour north of New York City in Putnam Valley, the lake was a popular getaway for ballplayers and sportswriters alike.

Lou and Babe examine Babe's five hundredth home run ball. Babe would go on to hit 714 home runs in his career, but Lou's total would stop at 493.

Lou felt the locker room was a quiet place to unwind in his hectic and increasingly high-pressure world.

Lou and Eleanor on their wedding day. Overwhelmed by the details of a large wedding, he convinced his fiancée to be married in a simple ceremony by the mayor of New Rochelle on September 29, 1933. Eleanor was Lou's first and only wife. They had no children.

Lou tagging Johnny Mize during an exhibition game in St. Petersburg. He never liked spring training in Florida, claiming that the bright sunshine hurt his eyes and affected his hitting.

Lou relaxing after a game with a cigarette and beer in 1936. His youthful objections to smoking and drinking had gradually changed over the years due to the influence of his teammates and wife.

Lou was thrown out in the fifth game of the 1936 World Series. On third base following a single and an error, he attempted, unsuccessfully, to score when his roommate, Bill Dickey, grounded out.

Hollywood came calling as Lou became more famous. Here Lou starred as a cowboy in the 1938 film *Rawhide*. One of Lou's teammates jokingly declared, "Gehrig was far and away the best first baseman now in the movies."

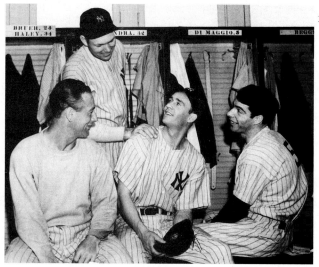

Lou at training camp in 1939. The other players, from left to right, are Bill Dickey, Joe Gordon, and Joe DiMaggio. The arm muscles that once gave Lou his driving force are no longer there.

The day Lou's streak ended. Although not yet diagnosed with ALS, Lou realized that he could no longer compete, so on May 2, 1939, he took himself out of the lineup and ended his streak of playing in 2,130 straight games. New York fans hoped that a little rest would restore his strength, but they would never see Lou Gehrig play baseball again.

Lou Gehrig Appreciation Day, July 4, 1939. The words from his farewell speech literally brought a nation to tears.

Lou studying for his new job on the New York City Parole Commission. He would find the work tremendously interesting and satisfying until his illness made him homebound.

Lou died at the age of thirty-seven on June 2, 1941. The next day, as accolades poured in, fans queued up for the official viewing at Christ Episcopal Church, just around the corner from Lou's home in the Bronx. Here, Babe Ruth paid his respects. After viewing Lou's body, Babe broke down and had to be led away to an anteroom to compose himself.

Lou Gehrig's legacy.

John Miljus showed us a good fastball and a curve that is as bothersome as any I've seen this year. No easy man to hit, this time, but having looked him over once, we may get to him. The number of pitchers who fooled the Yanks in the American League this year the first time they faced them is much larger than the number who fooled them the second time.

And my own part in the first game? Well, I nearly gummed the works in the third inning when Lazzeri and I started that attempt for a double steal. At that stage of the game, I was looking for a throw from [Earl] Smith to second base, and I was nicely crossed up when he threw to Traynor. I headed right for the plate then and managed, with the aid of Smith's error, to score, which was a good break for me.

Game 2
Yankees 6, Pirates 2

The Yanks have furnished, in part at least, the answer to the question concerning their effectiveness against a good curveball pitcher. Before the Series is over, the answer will be complete. Mind you, we aren't hitting up to our standard as yet, but in the second game of the World Series, all we did was to make eleven hits and six runs off Vic Aldridge, admittedly one of the best curveball pitchers in the National League, which as is generally accepted goes in for curveball pitching to a greater extent than our league does.

It is reasonable to suppose that when we do swing into our real form at the plate, we will make even better headway against all the curveballs the Pirates can fling at us. At that, yesterday's game wasn't such a bad demonstration of what we can do with a hook. Aldridge, as I have said, is one of the finest curveball pitchers in the league, and he had his curve with him in this game.

There was, however, one circumstance with which Aldridge had to contend that was strange to him. He never had pitched against the Yanks. I don't care whether a pitcher has a hook or a fastball or both. I don't care, for that matter, what he has. Pitching to the Yanks involves a greater strain mental and physical than that involved in pitching to any other club. The pitchers in our league could have told that to Aldridge. Maybe some of them did, but he had to find out about it first hand before he could appreciate it.

A pitcher of Aldridge's skill, facing the average ball club, finds that he can let down here and there along the line. No pitcher facing the Yanks can afford to let down anywhere along the line even when he comes to the pitchers. Why, Wilcy Moore is dangerous. I hope Wilcy doesn't read this, because he is inclined to be vain about that home run that he made this year, and I don't want to encourage him.

Seriously, though, this grind of pitching inning after inning to a lot of fellows who may knock the ball game out from under you at any minute is a tough assignment. In the first place, a pitcher is bound to be fearful that if he slips up just the slightest, somebody is going to lose the ball for him, and the burden of worry gets heavier instead of lighter as the innings roll by. In the second place, trying so hard to keep every ball where he wants it and bearing down all the times, he becomes physically tired.

The reason for Aldridge's weariness can be traced by looking at the score by innings of that second game. He was utterly worn out when they ushered him off the field in the eighth inning.

So far, I have written much about Aldridge and nothing about George Pipgras, who contributed one of the most magnificent games ever pitched in a World Series. He had everything, including confidence and control, which are as essential to a pitcher as his fast one and his hook. He was making his first appearance in a World Series game and pitching against one of the most dangerous hitting clubs in either league. But as near as I could tell by watching him closely, it was just a breeze for him. This didn't surprise any of us. We had seen George come along by leaps and bounds this year, and we knew at the end of the season that he was ready for the World Series. That's why we were so pleased when Miller Huggins told us he was going to pitch the second game. We wanted to see him get his chance; a little bit of sentiment we could afford to yield to because we knew that he would help us win.

The two victories we have scored give us a big edge in the Series, and while we still have a long way to go before we win it, I don't think the Pirates can head us off. In the first game, we had a few breaks in our favor and won because we made the most of them. There were no breaks for us yesterday, and we won. Anyhow, the method we used was identical with that which won for us in the opener. We hustled all the time from the moment we took the field until Joe Harris grounded to Pipgras for the last out. By hustling both in the field and on the bases, we kept on top of the Pirates all the way. The one run that Pittsburgh scored in the first inning didn't bother us. We knew we'd make more than that, and equally important we knew the Pirates would be lucky to make any more off Pipgras.

Game 3

Yankees 8, Pirates 1

Before the Series started, Miller Huggins said that if our pitchers were in form, we would beat the Pirates surely. In other words, that while the Yankees are best known as a great hitting ball club, our success in a Series with a club like the Pirates depended on our pitchers. Given high grade pitching, we could take care of ourselves very nicely.

All of which proves that Huggins knows what it's all about all the time. Our pitching has carried us to three victories in a row over the Pirates. In the first game, Waite Hoyt was not quite himself and couldn't do his usual stuff, but Wilcy Moore walked in when Waite had knocked off, and the Pirates were helpless. Then came George Pipgras with a wonderful exhibition and, following Pipgras, Herb Pennock.

I have seen Pennock pitch two games that stand out against the background of his usual pitching, brilliant as that is. One was a game he pitched against the Athletics on the Fourth of July, 1925, which was a shutout. The other was the game he pitched yesterday. In yesterday's game, he was as good as he ever was in his life, and I thought for a while—as everybody did—that he might hang up a no-hit game, which no pitcher ever has done in a World Series. I still think he might have done it but for our big inning in the seventh. Up to that time, the game had moved along swiftly, and Herb was loose and limber all the time. In the seventh, however, he had a long wait on the bench, during which he cooled out and, I believe, stiffened up just a trifle. That, if you ask me, is why the Pirates hit him harder in the last two innings.

Other features for our side were the hitting of a home run by Babe Ruth and the defensive play of Dugan, Koenig, and Lazzeri. I knew that homer of the Babe's couldn't be delayed much longer, the way he was swinging, and I felt it in my bones when he walked up there against Cvengros that poor Mike was about to take the rap, and what a smack that was! I could hear it whistle as I crouched near the plate waiting my turn to hit.

I never saw infield play to match that which we got from Joe, Mark, and Tony in this game. That bunt of [Harold] Rhyne's in the seventh was placed as prettily as a bunt could be. Rhyne was a one to a hundred shot when he left the plate—and a hundred to one when he was a stride from first base. Joe's a master of that stuff anyway, and he handled it perfectly. Koenig and Lazzeri both turned in some fine plays, the best of which were Mark's on [Forest] Wright in the eighth and Tony's on [Roy] Spencer in the same inning.

Lee Meadows is one of the best pitchers I ever looked at, even if we did beat him. Just as we beat Kremer and Aldridge. He has a good fastball and curve that is almost as fast—which helps to make it deceptive. A batter can't tell until the ball is right on top of him whether it's a fast one or a hook, and by the time he finds out, it may be too late. Meadows lacked only one thing to go through and give Pennock a tough fight right up to the end. That was the necessary stamina. Both pitchers were fine, but Meadows weakened and Pennock didn't. There, once more, was the unmistakable sign of the strain that goes into pitching against the Yankees.

Pie Traynor played a splendid game. I never have seen very much of him, but from what I had read about him, I regarded him as not only a first rate third baseman, but one of the greatest of all time, and that impression has been heightened by his work in this Series and particularly in yesterday's game.

We have the Pirates three down, and I do not see much chance for them to crowd in ahead of us. Yet it is too early to do any shouting. It has been proven time and again that a courageous ball club can work wonders even when the odds are piled high against it, and the Pirates have plenty of courage. They pulled through the National League race this year when they were sorely pressed and seemed about to go down, and though the count is against them, they must be regarded as a dangerous crowd.

Game 4

Yankees 4, Pirates 3

Wilcy Moore's pitching in the pinches, Babe Ruth's home run, and a tragic finish for Johnny Miljus—this is the story of the final World Series game.

Pitching hard all through the game, Moore came up with one of the gamest exhibitions of pitching he has given since he first put on a Yankee uniform, which is saying a great deal. For no pitcher ever showed more gameness in the tough spots than Cy did during the championship season. The conditions weren't exactly to his liking, with the field heavy and muddy and the ball damp much of the time, but he overcame these obstacles. Cy would have won much more easily than he did if it hadn't been for that play on Earl Smith in the seventh inning.

I fielded the ball and made a long toss to Cy as he crossed the bag, but he failed to hold the ball, and Smith was safe. It was a hard play to make, and I wish he could have got through with it all right, because if he had, I am sure he would not have been scored upon in that inning. However, it didn't prevent us from winning the game and served only to show Cy at his best as a relief pitcher in the next two innings.

Babe's homer was great. I have seen him make many a one since I joined the club, and each of them has given me a thrill, but I never expected to get a greater thrill than I did when the Babe boosted that ball high and far into the bleachers. It was a terrific blow to the Pirates, and that they were able to tie the score and force us to go into the ninth inning to win the game is another indication of their courage.

I believe that, glad as we were to win the Series, every man on our club felt sorry for Miljus at the finish. John had gotten into a bad jam at the very start of the inning, and the intentional pass he was ordered to give to Babe filled the bases with none out. Then he turned on extra stuff and, after striking me out, did the same to Meusel. This put it up to Lazzeri, and we were rooting hard for Tony on the bench when Miljus lost control of the ball, let it go for a wild pitch, and sent Combs over the plate with the winning run.

It meant a victory for us, but it was a heart-breaker for Miljus, and we couldn't help regret that the game had ended in that fashion. If we had won on a hit by Lazzeri, we would not have been sympathetic, of course, for that sort of thing is all a part of the game. I am sure Tony would have smacked one if he had had the opportunity.

Carmen Hill, like the Pirate pitchers who had preceded him, is a splendid pitcher and had a lot of stuff, plus plenty of nerve. No pitcher ever got out of a tight fix in better style than he did in the first inning, and he was going along great until the Babe lost the ball for him in the fifth.

There were a lot of happy ballplayers in our clubhouse last evening. We were all talking at once, telling each other how good we were, and when the door opened and in walked Barney Dreyfuss, he shook hands first with Miller Huggins and then with the rest of us, being very generous in his praise. He is a real sportsman, and we all wish him a lot of luck for 1928. And that goes, too, for Donie Bush, a great little fellow and a fine manager. They have a splendid ball club there, even if they couldn't beat us this year.

World Series Summary

World Series in other years have developed arguments as to whether or not the better club won, but I do not think there is even elbow room for an argument on that point this year.

The Pirates, having won the National League pennant in a courageous dash, unquestionably have plenty of class, but they were not a match for the Yankees. We won by grace of superior pitching, timely hitting, and a fine defense. There were no breaks for either team, taking the Series by and large.

We simply won because we had more stuff than the Pirates. The first game was the loosest of the Series mainly because it was the first game. By that, I mean that both clubs were over anxious, and before they settled down, the game was about over, with the Yanks in front. Neither Waite Hoyt, who started for us, nor Ray Kremer, who opposed him, was at his best. The relief pitching in that game, offered by Wilcy Moore for us and John Miljus for the Pirates, was fine.

The Series proved, I think, that the two major leagues are well balanced. We ran away with the race in the American League, and, on the assumption that the leagues are well balanced, we figured to win the Series from the Pirates, who had won the National League pennant only after a hard fight. That is exactly what happened.

We beat the National League champions just as we had beaten clubs in our league in every important series we had played. The Series also proved, among other things, that the Yankees can hit curveball pitching. We batted against Aldridge, Meadows, and Hill, whose curves rank with the best in the National League, known among ballplayers as a curveball league, and none of the three could go the route against us. And, finally, it proved that the Pirates can be beaten by a left-handed pitcher, provided the left-handed pitcher is a Pennock.

I think the players on our club have every reason to be satisfied with the work they did in the Series. No man stood out, but every man buckled down to the task of taking four games in a row from the Pirates, and every man did his share. I was especially glad to see Mark Koenig shine.

Poor Mark was suffering with bothersome injuries a year ago and could not do his best against the Cardinals. He felt this very keenly and was so eager to hang up a good performance this year that he had us all pulling harder for him, perhaps, than for any other man on the club.

Chapter 9

And now I come to the end of my story of my baseball experience.

And in closing, I want to say just this: I am proud to be a big league ballplayer and proud to associate with the men who make professional baseball. I believe that baseball is a real profession, worthy of the best that any man can give. In my experience as a ballplayer, I have found nothing to be ashamed of, nothing that was not within the bounds of good judgment and good sportsmanship.

I gave up college to take up baseball—and I do not consider my efforts wasted. I'm glad I attended college, and I'm proud to be known as a college man. But I don't subscribe to the old-fashioned idea that a college man belittles himself when he goes in for a career of college athletics.

I don't believe I would have met a finer group of men anywhere than I have met in baseball. Nor a squarer, fairer lot of men, either.

Of course, I am just a kid at the game, and I realize it. I still have much to learn, and I hope I still have many years in which to learn it. But this I do know, that baseball is today and will be the greatest game in the world. And if I ever get married and have any sons who show promise of real baseball ability, I can only hope that professional baseball will offer them as much as it has offered me, and treat them as kindly.

As for the years that lie ahead, I can only hope for the best. If I succeed or if I fall, if I'm a star or a flop, there can at least be this said: I'll give the best I have, play the best I can, do the best I can. And that, I think, is the spirit of every man in professional baseball today.

It has been my good fortune to break into the game at a time when some of the greatest of all stars were playing. There will never be another Babe Ruth. He stands alone and incomparable. And I doubt if there will ever be another Ty Cobb.

But there will always be great ballplayers so long as kids can find sandlots on which to mark off a diamond; and baseball can never grow less honorable so long as those same kids look to the big league stars as their heroes.

One thing I'd like to see. I'm looking forward to the time when more and more college men will find their way into the ranks of professional baseball. I believe that college men can contribute much to the good of the game—and it's a certain cinch that baseball can contribute much to the welfare and the benefit of the college man. When I came into baseball, I was a green kid who knew nothing about the game.

Older men befriended me and helped me and advised me. I will never forget their kindness. And perhaps someday I'll have a chance to repay them by passing that same advice and that same aid on to youngsters who come along while I am a regular.

I hope I may be able to do just that.

But regardless of whether I do or not, regardless of whether I succeed or fail, let this be my final promise.

I'm proud to be a ballplayer. I'm proud of the game and the men who play it. And so long as I wear a big league uniform, I will give all I can to the game.

Lou

The Biographical Essay

ALAN D. GAFF

Early Years

Henry Louis Gehrig was born June 19, 1903, in a four-story apartment building at 309 East Ninety-Fourth Street in the borough of Manhattan in New York City. Lou would later recall, "I had two sisters and a brother, and we were a sickly lot and caught everything. We were all down at one time, and though Mother did everything possible, I alone survived." Lou's father, Heinrich Gehrig, left Adelheim, Germany, in 1888 in search of the promise of America. Lou's mother, Christina Fack, a native of Wiltster, Germany, reached the United States eleven years later. Not long after meeting, Heinrich and Christina were married in New York City on November 27, 1900. Lou would say of them, "My mother and father were hardworking people, and they hadn't had great educational advantages. But they were American parents, willing to work hard and skimp to give their son the advantages that they had missed."

Both of Lou's parents were German speakers, "big-boned, strong, and ambitious." His mother doted on Lou. She recalled, "I don't pretend Lou was born with a silver spoon in his mouth. But he never left the table hungry, and I can say he had a terrible appetite from the first time he saw daylight. Maybe his clothes were torn, dirty, and rumpled after playing baseball and football, but he always was clean and neatly dressed when I sent him off to school." When the chunky blond kid with the ever-present blue cap set off with his schoolbooks every morning, he did so with a full stomach. Mom Gehrig invariably filled him up with milk, toast, and jam alongside a half dozen eggs, this feast often being augmented by stacks of German or buckwheat pancakes. Lou's tremendous appetite would amaze onlookers for the rest of his life.

Heinrich Gehrig occasionally found work at $9 or $10 per week as an ornamental ironworker, crafting grilles, railings, and balustrades. Work was sporadic, so he spent most of his time at the local Turnverein, a social club where German Americans would exercise, drink beer, and play cards. Lou used to tag along and use the equipment: parallel bars, pommel horse, pulleys, and weights. Young Gehrig would not learn English until he entered Public School 132 at the age of five.

The Gehrigs lived in several apartments in Yorkville, a clannish colony of Germans and eastern Europeans established in the 1790s. Wedged between the East Side and Spanish Harlem, Yorkville was like a small piece of the German fatherland in New York City. Immigrants had been drawn to the district by jobs available at Ruppert Brewery, run by none other than Jacob Ruppert, Lou's future employer as owner of the New York Yankees. Pushcarts roamed the streets offering staples and seasonal fruits and vegetables. Everyone worked six days a week, many families taking in single boarders to make ends meet. Recreation centered on the numerous beer gardens, with parades, yodeling, songfests, and dancing.

Mom Gehrig soon saved enough money to move the family

north to an apartment in Washington Heights. She would bristle whenever she read that Lou had been brought up in the New York slums and learned to play baseball in the streets. She declared: "From the time Lou was five in 1908 until he was graduated from grade school in 1917, he attended Public School Number 132, at One Hundred Eighty-Second Street and Wadsworth Avenue. This is in a good residential section of Washington Heights, and anyone residing in that locality properly would resent it being called the slums."

Looking back as an adult, Lou would remember, "I was a poor kid. We lived in a poor neighborhood. But it was in America, where even poor kids in poor neighborhoods got good breaks— playgrounds, supervised athletics, good public schools." In a belated apology to his mother, he also admitted to having been a rebellious child: "I wasn't old enough in those days to appreciate what she was doing, and I was a pretty bad kid. I raised the devil in every way imaginable and did not miss a single trick."

When he was a youngster, neighborhood kids never picked Lou when choosing their sports teams. Besides not speaking English, Lou was so fat and clumsy that other boys would tease him, push him around, and often chase him home. Relegated to the sidelines, he would watch impromptu baseball games only as a spectator, staring intently as boys threw, hit, and caught a small leather ball, occasionally running between stuffed gunnysacks.

When they learned that Lou was a good swimmer, boys who had shunned him on the baseball fields now enjoyed having him along, piling their clothes on shore while they splashed in the Hudson River. Lou's favorite swimming hole was around the old masonry pillars of High Bridge, which connected Manhattan and the Bronx. It was a long trek but well worth the walk during hot summer months. At the age of eleven, Lou swam the Hudson River only to be punished for such a reckless stunt. One other time, Heinrich had to go to the police station to retrieve his son, who had been taken into custody for swimming without trunks in the Harlem River. After swimming all day and missing supper, Lou admitted that they would "get the devil whaled out of us for waywardness."

Schoolmates who refused to have Lou on their baseball teams had been won over after swimming with him in the Hudson. While he might have had trouble with his schoolwork, Lou soon became a fixture on the PS 132 baseball team in Washington Heights. He played first base and would occasionally pitch, although he could do little more than throw hard. His unfulfilled dream was to be a catcher, despite being left-handed. As a hitter, Lou was enthusiastic but dreadful. He would swing hard at every pitch, teammates complaining that he "kept one foot in the water bucket," meaning to act timidly at bat by stepping away from the plate with his lead foot.

Gehrig expanded his horizons by playing on neighborhood diamonds at Bennett Field and Reservoir Oval. Still introverted and uncomfortable around strangers even his own age, Lou would show up for a game in tired old clothes and shoes, borrowing a glove or a bat, but always with a smile on his face. Lou was no different from millions of other kids across America who played baseball in parks, sandlots, and in the streets. The young Gehrig began to work off his baby fat, replacing it with muscles that led to more ability in sports.

Lou Gehrig did not emerge unscathed from his childhood.

Although he became huskier and stronger than other boys, he never was acknowledged as a leader. Despite his growing skill in athletics, Irish kids generally led the spontaneous activities, Lou still being called "Dutchman" or "Krauthead." A close friend would remember, "He was shy, timid, with an early inferiority complex." Paul Gallico, one of Lou's biographers, explained, "Early in life, he became imbued with a sense of his own worthlessness, which he never overcame to the end of his days. He just never understood how he could possibly be any good, or how anybody could really love or care for him. . . . As a man, his greatest handicap was that he was super sensitive, shy, self-accusing, quick to take hurt, and slow to recover therefrom." Christina's smothering affection for Lou eventually led, according to American sportswriter Fred Lieb, to a sort of Oedipus complex between the pair.

Christina stressed her son's education so that he would not end up as a butcher or carpenter, and Lou did all he could to appease her. Homework was completed immediately after school, and his attendance record was perfect. Heinrich pitched in to help with math problems, his proficiency no doubt related to numerous hours of playing pinochle in the Turnverein. Yet still, Lou was never an outstanding student. He was a worse baseball player, known in school as "a left-handed catcher who couldn't hit the length of his cap." It seems the only thing Lou was really good at was delivering the laundry that his mother bundled for her customers.

After he graduated from PS 132 in 1917, Christina insisted that her son enroll in the High School of Commerce, hoping he could become an architect or civil engineer. Foregoing his growing passion for baseball, Lou spent the first year concentrating on his studies. He remained a bit of an outsider, being laughed at for wearing knee-length pants. Gehrig bought a pair of long pants with his scanty savings and hid them from his mother. Every school day, he would place his long pants in the dumbwaiter, retrieve them downstairs, and pull them over his short pants. After a day of study, Lou would take off his long pants, send them back up the dumbwaiter, and hide them for the next day. He often walked or hitched a ride on a delivery wagon to save bus fare. One boy in his class remembered, "No one who went to school with Lou can forget the cold winter days and Lou coming to school wearing khaki shirt, khaki pants, and heavy brown shoes, but no overcoat, nor any hat. He was a poor boy." He seemed to be always "embarrassed that he didn't have any clothes or any money to treat anybody to an occasional soft drink or cone."

While Lou had eschewed baseball during his first year, he had reluctantly been coaxed onto the school soccer team. A freshman named Oliver Gintel one day kicked the ball toward Gehrig, who casually booted it across the practice field. Gintel urged Lou to join the soccer team, but he bashfully admitted he was no good at sports and confessed that his mother would never consent to such a distraction. After he refused the coach's recruitment, Lou was denounced as lacking school spirit, being called a sissy and a mama's boy.

When Lou convinced his mother that soccer would not get in the way of his schoolwork, he somewhat nervously joined the team. He played three successful years as a halfback (now midfielder), winning three winter championships in a row.

Baseball coach Alfred DuSchatko heard of Lou's prowess on

the soccer field and insisted that he try out for the team. Skipping tryouts, Lou showed up to practice in street clothes and shoes, not having so much as spikes or a glove. DuSchatko gave him a uniform and equipment, with orders to report for a game at Lewisohn Stadium, a huge eight-thousand-seat amphitheater in Harlem. Engrossed in his bookkeeping textbook, Lou rode past his subway stop. Realizing his mistake, he got off and began to walk to the stadium while still reading. Before he could join his team, a roar from the crowd stopped him in his tracks. Intimidated by the scene, Lou ran for home and handed in his uniform the next day. But Coach DuSchatko convinced Lou to return, aided by a threat from his bookkeeping teacher to fail him if he did not join the lineup. Lou finally experienced game play as a first baseman in 1917. He was fourteen.

Despite modest success on the soccer field, Lou's real passion was baseball, although he did not play well. He was later described at this period by Paul Gallico as "a poor performer on the diamond." His greatest attribute was to sporadically hit a baseball a long way, one high school student recalling that "if you happened to play in a class game against him and he knocked the ball over your head, you just ran after it." Sadly for Lou, this happened all too infrequently.

Misfortune struck the Gehrig household when Heinrich became seriously ill, which left him a semi-invalid the rest of his life. Mom took on more work to support her family, while Lou pitched in with weekend jobs at a corner grocery and butcher shop. He also found employment at the Alpha Chi Rho fraternity house on the Columbia University campus, doing whatever needed to be done. A summer job with the Otis Elevator Company allowed him to play in a Yonkers city league. One day his temper flashed at a bad call, leading to a fistfight with an umpire. Although Lou would argue with umpires over calls in the future, he never again got into a physical confrontation over a disputed decision.

The High School of Commerce baseball team defeated the Commercial High School team from Brooklyn for the unofficial high school city title on June 18, 1920. Lou contributed two doubles and a walk in four at bats. As a result, the squad was invited to Chicago to play the best high school team the Windy City had to offer. Special railroad cars with deluxe accommodations would carry the team westward, with all expenses shared by the *Daily News* and the *Chicago Tribune*. But when Lou rushed home with the news that he was going to Chicago, his parents were unimpressed. Mom called it "foolishness," while Heinrich said it was nothing but "monkey shines." Lou would later explain, "They talked about it well into the night. It was as though I was going to Borneo or Zanzibar. Finally, they decided if the school would be responsible for me during my absence, they would grant their consent." It was the first time that Mom loosened the apron strings on her precious boy.

A photograph of Lou and two teammates appeared in the *New York Daily News*, an impressive achievement for a high school player. As a show of support, Brooklyn Dodgers owner Charles Ebbets allowed coach Harry Kane's boys to practice at his club's Ebbets Field—their first steps onto a major league diamond. More than a thousand supporters accompanied their buses to the train depot, and the *Daily News* again carried a photograph of Lou, this one showing him at batting practice.

Kane's team refused a tour of the city in favor of watching a game between the Chicago White Sox and the Cleveland Indians. When the two high school teams met on June 26 at Cubs Park, there was a World Series atmosphere, with bands, cheerleaders, photographers, reporters, motion picture cameras, and a jazz band to play between innings for a crowd of ten thousand. Lou's team was ahead 8–6 when he came to bat in the top of the ninth inning with two outs and the bases loaded. Gehrig took a fastball. Then he slammed the second pitch over the right field wall to clear the bases. Sportswriters compared his dramatic home run to those being hit by Babe Ruth, one exclaiming breathlessly, "The real Babe never poled one more thrilling." After celebrating their victory, Kane's ballplayers boarded an eastbound train back to New York, where they were greeted by more than five thousand fans. Gehrig's feat was widely reported, although his surname was often misspelled and his photograph misidentified. After basking in this brief glow of fame, Lou Gehrig put on his old clothes, went back to school, and resumed supporting his family.

Columbia University to
Yankee Stadium

After graduation on January 27, 1921, Lou enrolled in Columbia University's extension program to make up for some scholastic deficiencies until he entered the freshman class in September. But his grand slam in Chicago had caught the attention of the New York Giants, a perennial challenger for the National League title. As the baseball season commenced, Manager John McGraw and scout Arthur Devlin thought that this long-ball hitter deserved a look, so Gehrig was invited to show his stuff at the Polo Grounds, home of the Giants in Upper Manhattan. He exhibited promise as a hitter but was so clumsy fielding that McGraw dismissed him as unteachable. Although Lou had already practiced with the Columbia baseball squad, Giants scouts recommended that he get more experience with the Hartford Senators in the Eastern League, assuring him that it would not interfere with his college baseball career. Lou moved to Hartford and played briefly under the not too subtle name "Lew Lewis," appearing in just a dozen games, hitting only .261. When Andy Coakley, manager of the Columbia Lions, learned what Gehrig was doing, he traveled to Hartford and yanked the eighteen-year-old off the team. For this short stint of playing for a professional organization, Lou was suspended from all collegiate sports for a year.

Gehrig could at least practice with the football and baseball squads. His suspension lifted in time for the 1922 football season. He was slated to play tackle on the varsity team until he complained to coach Frank "Buck" O'Neill that he wanted to carry the ball. Words were passed between player and coach, and Lou was asked to turn in his uniform. O'Neill called him "stubborn and bull-headed" but ultimately relented, and Gehrig was reinstated as a fullback to start the season.

While he enjoyed athletics, Lou never fit in socially at Columbia. He joined the Phi Delta Theta fraternity, but his acceptance was based on his being an athlete, not his social status. Biographer Paul Gallico explained that "freshmen who looked as though they might someday become star athletes and shed their light upon their brothers were plums, and Lou Gehrig was a plum deluxe. They took him in, not because they wanted to, but because they had to. If they hadn't, another fraternity would have." He was a fraternity brother in name only because they all knew his mother was only a cook, while their parents came from the upper class. Lou felt used, and he was, "being in the college and playing for the college, but never actually being *of* the college." Gallico explained his painful situation: "He withdrew still further within himself. He became more shy and self-accusing. He was convinced that he was no good for anything and never would be."

As practice began for the 1923 baseball season, Coach Coakley found himself with an awkward athlete with potential. By the end of the 1922 football season, Lou had bulked up to nearly

240 pounds, so Coakley put him on a strict diet and exercise program. The coach had no idea where to fit young Gehrig into his lineup. He tried the outfield, but Lou had trouble catching fly balls. Coakley then tried the young man as a pitcher. He had a decent fastball and acceptable curveball but lacked control. Lou confessed that in practice he was "wild enough nearly to decapitate some of the best players on the Columbia team." As if to prove his point, in a game against Williams College, he struck out seventeen batters but lost 5–1 after walking too many opponents.

Lou settled in at first base. Coach Coakley, a graduate of Holy Cross and a former major-league pitcher, spent countless hours hitting grounders to improve Lou's fielding. Coakley's mantra was "stop a ball, throw it straight, and get base hits." Sensing Gehrig's potential as a hitter, he emphasized the fundamentals: keep close to the plate and avoid pulling the ball. A student at Columbia would recall "seeing a lumbering, awkward kid out there in the evening shadows shagging flies and banging a dirty old baseball lopsided until the shades of night either drove him home or obscured him." Lou did everything with enthusiasm, whether it be baseball or combing his always immaculate hair. Coakley remembered, "When there were no varsity games or practices to take up his time, he could be spotted in pickup games on the campus—playing just as hard as if he were in a World Series."

Off the field, Coach Coakley had no established rules, explaining that the more rules he laid down, the more that would be broken. In his words, this lenient system meant "the worst thing they do is drink too many ice cream sodas." Switching between first base and pitcher, Gehrig began to flourish under Coakley's tutelage. When the coach invited New York sportswriter Hugh

Fullerton to observe his emerging slugger, Fullerton concluded that Gehrig could become another Babe Ruth, assuming he could hit major-league pitching. He explained: "I have seen him hit a ball into the center field stands—which are 418 feet from the plate, 20 feet high, and 30 feet deep." By the first week in May, Lou was hitting .540 and had struck out 44 men in the four games he pitched. Having slimmed down to just over two hundred pounds, he could run a hundred yards in eleven seconds.

Paul Krichell, a scout for the New York Yankees, chanced to see Lou hit two home runs in a game against Rutgers College on April 26, 1923. Paul telephoned headquarters to announce that he'd found the next Babe Ruth. Krichell was on hand to watch Gehrig's next game, this one against Connecticut's Wesleyan in mid-May. Not only did Lou pitch a three-hitter, but also he smashed the longest home run ever seen on the Columbia ball field. Krichell grabbed Andy Coakley after the game and headed for the locker room, where, after brief introductions, the scout offered Lou an opportunity to play for the Yankees.

The next day, Lou, Coakley, and Krichell met in the office of Ed Barrow, the Yankees business manager. Lou described the encounter later: "My dad hadn't worked for five months, and my mother was in a hospital with double pneumonia. Eight clubs were bidding for me, but the house of Gehrig was broke. Ed Barrow waved $1,500 in front of me, and I grabbed it so quick that I'll bet he never saw it change hands." That sum was a relatively modest signing bonus, with a starting salary of $400 a month. Gehrig discovered later that Coakley had received $500 of his $1,500 as a finder's fee—a third of his bonus—a fact that briefly soured their relationship. Lou explained to a friend his reasoning for signing his first Yankees contract: "Mom's been slaving to put me, a young ox, twenty years old and weighing around two hundred pounds, through college. Well, it's about time that I carry the load and take care of them. I've signed with the Yankees, said good-bye to Columbia, and from now on, all my thoughts are on a successful career in baseball." Lou's college career was over, leaving his mother distraught that he would never become an engineer.

Lou Gehrig joined the Yankees for a practice session on June 11, 1923. Pitcher Waite Hoyt remembered the day: "He was big, not an oversize athlete, but the lean kind of big. We were all standing around the batting cage when Lou came out with Miller Huggins. He was a nervous-looking boy." The veterans watched the new arrival carefully: "Gehrig stood around with us, and then Huggins told him to get a bat. I remember seeing him stand in there waiting for the juicy pitches. One, two, three, four times he swung, and the catcher caught every one."

Lou soon settled down: "Then he tagged one, a screaming liner, and everyone around watched it dip to left-center field. He smacked another one, and then he belted one into the stands. The pressure was off." After batting practice, Lou headed to the outfield to shag flies, leaving his new teammates to agree that the new kid had potential.

The Yankees had won the 1921 and 1922 American League pennants but been beaten in the World Series by their longtime nemesis the Giants both times. Now, for the first time, the Yankees were playing home games in their own ballpark, having previously shared the Polo Grounds with the Giants. Yankee Stadium opened on April 18, 1923, boasting a steel-and-concrete grandstand, with wooden bleachers surrounding the outfield. There was a press box directly behind home plate and an immense scoreboard in center field. It was a new era for the team, the atmosphere that day being compared to "a super world series." The Yankees celebrated the grand opening of their new home by beating the Red Sox 4–1, Babe Ruth christening the right field bleachers with a home run before 74,200 fans. This auspicious start began what has been acknowledged as a dynasty in the American League that lasted for an unprecedented four more decades.

The legendary Miller Huggins was manager when Lou reported to the Yankees after the conclusion of his sophomore year at Columbia. Huggins was noted for his knowledge of baseball fundamentals and was an ardent student of the game, emphasizing bunts, sacrifice flies, and base stealing prior to the arrival of Babe Ruth. According to one insider, "He wanted players with spunk, eagerness for work, a capacity for learning, appreciation for decency, and, of course, ability." Above all else, Huggins insisted on signing players with "proper dispositions." His well-known patience with young players allowed him to develop raw talent that had been passed over by other teams. So it was with Lou, who greatly appreciated a chance to prove himself.

Sportswriter Marshall Hunt recalled how critics of Huggins called him a "crab, a dour-faced grouch, and a spineless manager." He was never popular with the fans. However, his soft-spoken approach eventually won over even the most "egocentric, surly, and refractory athletes," including the most boisterous of them all, Babe Ruth, who had become "bigger than baseball," according to Marshall Hunt. The Bambino liked to break curfew, stay out all night, sign in at the clubhouse just before dawn, and sleep until noon. In 1925 Huggins fined his star the astronomical sum of $5,000 for ignoring every team rule. Babe's transition to a Huggins-type player can be seen in his own words. In 1925 he stated, "Huggins can't manage his own garters." Two years later, Babe would admit, "Huggins is a pretty nice little feller." In 1928 Ruth bragged, "Huggins is a helluva good manager." As opposed to Ruth's gradual conversion, Lou was a Huggins fan from the beginning, one friend writing of Lou's loyalty, "Gehrig would have jumped through fire, charged a runaway freight train, if Huggins had ordered it."

Lou would soon discover that being on a major-league team did not mean actually playing in games. As one writer explained, "He warmed the bench. He watched the other players. He pitched in the bullpen. He shagged flies, hit fungoes. He did everything but play in a game." When Mom and Pop Gehrig came to Yankee Stadium to see their son play, he remained in the dugout all afternoon. That night at dinner, Pop wanted to know where he had been hiding. Lou said he had been sitting on the bench, to which Pop asked how a man could make $400 a month just sitting on a bench. It did not make sense to either of his parents, but the money was good.

Huggins finally put Lou in the lineup on June 18 to pinch-hit against the Detroit Tigers, who led in the ninth inning by eight runs. He struck out. Lou got another chance to bat on July 2, facing John "Bonnie" Hollingsworth of the Washington Senators. He whiffed on three fastballs. Sitting down next to Babe Ruth in the dugout, the twenty-year-old was surprised to hear, "Never you mind, kid. You'll pickle one next time. You took your cuts anyway. You didn't just stand there and watch the balls go by." Tears came to his eyes at these words of encouragement. Lou took advantage of his next chance in a game lost to the St. Louis Browns, 13–3. Looking good enough to be in advertisements and boasting a body that resembled "the slim, delicate lines of a railroad locomotive," according to biographer Richard Hubler, Gehrig singled to right field.

After watching Lou at practice and in limited playing time, Huggins reached a decision: Lou Gehrig had the raw talent and the will to become a great ballplayer. The Yankees' manager remarked, "When he came here, he didn't know a thing; he was one of the dumbest players I've ever seen. But he's got one great virtue that will make him: he never makes the same mistake twice. He makes all the mistakes, all right, but not twice." What Lou needed was "seasoning," a year or two in the minors to work through his defects by playing every day rather than sitting on the Yankees' bench. On August 1 Huggins sent Lou to finish the season in the Eastern League at Hartford, where he had played before losing his collegiate eligibility. Lou's dreams of playing for the Yankees had been crushed. One biographer said, "If someone had offered him any kind of job at that moment, he would have taken it." But with no other prospects and no longer eligible to resume his athletic career at Columbia, Lou had no choice but to pack his bags and head for Hartford.

The Minors

Although glum at the prospect of leaving the Yankees, Lou appreciated a chance to play every day. He was on a streak, hitting homers and winning games. All seemed finally to be going well. Then came a sharp decline. For two weeks, Lou played badly. Part of the problem may have been a deep spike cut on his leg resulting from a collision with a runner along the baseline at first. Lou never would have used the injury as an excuse, but the fact remained that he was in a terrible batting slump.

Depressed to see his career evaporate in front of him, Lou went out drinking with his teammates despite the country being in its fourth year of Prohibition. He had more than his share of bootleg gin and arrived at the ballpark, as he later told Paul Gallico, feeling like "the cold clinkers of hell." Despite being hung over, Gehrig ended his slump with some hard smashes. Some even noticed that he played first base with "elegance and ease," two words that had never been used to describe Lou's fielding. Thinking he had found his baseball fountain of youth, Lou began to buy more liquor, again confessing to Gallico that "it tasted horrible and made his mouth feel like the inside of a second baseman's glove." He even hid small bottles of booze in his uniform, taking a sip now and then in the dugout.

Pat O'Connor soon discovered young Gehrig's secret and pulled him in for a conversation. The coach started, "What the hell is going on here, Lou?" He launched into a lecture about hanging with the wrong crowd, men whose careers had been destroyed by drink. O'Connor continued, "Maybe you're just a big, dumb Dutchman, but I think you've got a chance to go places in baseball, or I wouldn't be wasting my time here talking to you." Lou acted surprised at the coach's accusation, explaining away his newfound success by saying, "I just came on it by accident." O'Connor brushed aside this childish explanation and explained how badly alcohol could impede his career. Gehrig took O'Connor's advice and would avoid hard liquor in the future, realizing that it could be poison in his line of work. Lou would refer to this period of his life as the two-week drunk.

Senators fans had grown to love their German American slugger. Hailed as "one of the greatest attractions in minor league baseball," he "made friends galore and put himself in a position where every move he makes will be followed by Hartford baseball lovers." He departed the city when recalled to the Yankees that fall, with Huggins inserting Lou at first base after longtime starter Wally Pipp twisted his ankle hopping off a train. Lou announced his arrival with a home run and three doubles. Huggins wanted to keep him for the 1923 World Series; however, Judge Kenesaw Mountain Landis, baseball's first commissioner, declared he would leave that decision up to the opposing manager. John McGraw of the Giants refused to accept Lou as a substitute for Pipp, so after appearing in just six games and being ineligible for World Series play, Lou was sent back to Hartford.

After the season, the Yankees organization let it be known

that Gehrig would remain in the minors for all of 1924, earning him the nicknames "the Bambino's understudy" and "Columbia Lou." Paul Krichell said that Lou would be worth $100,000 to the right team. But the Yankees had no intention of letting him go to another club. There was speculation that returning to Hartford might be complicated, but Lou made it clear that "if he must go a minor-leaguing, he'd rather be in Hartford than any other place."

While he waited for the 1924 season, Lou worked for an electric company and spent several days a week that fall helping Harry Kane coach his old high school baseball team. This was not the era of million-dollar contracts. By February, he'd quit the job to assist Andy Coakley at Columbia, Gehrig apparently having forgiven him for taking a hefty cut of Lou's signing bonus with the Yankees.

When various American League teams refused to grant waivers allowing Lou Gehrig to play a second year in Hartford, Miller Huggins declared, "They won't let me put the kid out in the minors, eh? Well, then, I'll just let him play in the majors right with the Yankees, probably in the outfield." Adding the hard-slugging Gehrig to an outfield already boasting Babe Ruth and Bob Meusel would threaten other clubs enough to allow Lou to clear waivers and return to the Senators in 1924.

But first Lou joined the Yankees at training camp in New Orleans. Sportswriter Bill Corum wrote that the young man left New York on February 28, 1924, with "12 bucks in his pocket, hope in his heart." Upon his arrival, one of the regulars asked to borrow $10, so Lou gave it to him to avoid looking cheap. In New Orleans, Lou did not say much and did not spend much. His future wife would later recall, "The other Yankees regarded Lou as something of a young tightwad because he was still the austere Boy Scout type who didn't do much drinking except for a beer or two and who didn't suffer many temptations from the high life. He simply had never acquired the habit of spending money, even after he began to earn it." Lou would walk from Heinemann Park to the team hotel to save paying for a taxi. After having expended his last $2, he took a part-time job as a soda jerk to pay for his incidental expenses until Huggins found out about it and advanced him extra expense money.

Players slept in until eight o'clock, then watched Lou put away a massive breakfast. Said to be "highly skilled in the art of wielding a devastating left-hand knife and fork," he ate more than anyone else on the team. An observer noted, "In the matter of sustenance, Mr. Gehrig is no bargain to any ball club." One reason for his hearty appetite was that he skipped lunch after finding he was expected to leave a tip. His gargantuan passion for food, even away from Christina's home cooking, led reporters to call him "Hungry Lou Gehrig" and "Biscuit Pants." It was a Gehrig family tradition to eat massive meals. Between Pop and Mom and Lou, the Gehrigs tipped the scale at a combined 675 pounds. Mom claimed, "It takes a lot of fuel to keep us going."

Packed to the brim at breakfast, Lou began to treat New Orleans spectators to hitting "of the Ruthian variety." With Babe Ruth suffering from influenza in Hot Springs, Arkansas, Lou Gehrig would provide the mighty blasts that people had expected to see. Yet there was still the problem of fielding, now magnified by a tendency to catch the ball too close to his body on throws to first base.

Few of those trying out for the team in New Orleans would make the cut, although they were good enough to make the grade on other major-league clubs. Sportswriter Marshall Hunt explained, "They tried to break into a formidable lineup which is not yet ready to be torn apart." When American League clubs saw they had no chance of snatching Lou from the Yankees, they withdrew their objections, allowing him to return to Connecticut. With Wally Pipp healthy and Manager Huggins satisfied with his outfield, Gehrig was sent back to play a second year for Pat O'Connor at Hartford.

On opening day, April 25, 1924, "Lefty Lou" picked up where he had left off the previous year, with the stands full of fans waiting to see him blast one. He did not disappoint and hit one over the right field fence in the first inning against New Haven. Lou would hit home runs out of every ballpark in the Eastern League. By the time of his last game with Hartford on August 30, he had racked up 37 home runs, 13 triples, 40 doubles, and led the Eastern League with a .369 batting average.

Gehrig remained the franchise's favorite player. Even when he went hitless in his final home game, Lou received a rousing round of applause each time he stepped to the plate. His last act as a Hartford Senator was to make the final putout in the ninth inning before tossing the ball into the stands. Although Hartford would not repeat as conference champion, Lou Gehrig had left his mark. Described as "a stunningly handsome boy with wavy, brown hair, and dimples in his cheeks," Lou looked like a god in his baseball uniform. When he smiled, it was said to resemble "Shirley Temple's dimples on a mountain." The young man loved steak, movies, and music, although he was disqualified from an impromptu Senatorial quartet "after a trial lasting six seconds." Girls swooned over him until they learned how cheap he could be and how dowdy he looked in his patched, rumpled clothes.

Lou was called up again to the Yankees by Miller Huggins as insurance in what proved to be a failed run for the 1924 American League pennant. He first appeared as a pinch hitter on August 31 but did not reach base. Lou would play in 12 games and go 6 for 12 with a double and 5 singles. A perceptive writer for the *Hartford Courant* summed up Gehrig's 1924 transition, noting that his hitting had become more consistent, but the ratio of home runs to at bats had fallen slightly. His problems fielding still remained, and the twenty-one-year-old was a terrible base runner whose inability to think quickly and understand a situation led to him being caught between bases. Despite Gehrig's obvious flaws and not yet being a finished player, Miller Huggins expected him to be a cash cow in New York during the 1925 season. Yankees management almost salivated at the prospect of Babe Ruth and Lou Gehrig in the same lineup. In such a case, according to a Hartford writer, "The baseball factories would have to put on double shifts making enough baseballs to keep up with the demand."

To prepare himself for 1925 spring training, Lou Gehrig enrolled in the Savage School of Physical Education, an institution devoted to physical culture, in October after the baseball season. His reasons were twofold: he was determined to keep in shape and, tired of living away from home for most of the year, he missed Mom's home cooking.

A Yankee Again

After lousy weather and distracting social activities in New Orleans, Jacob Ruppert decreed that spring training in 1925 needed to be held somewhere else. In the Yankees' owner's words, "We got to get the team to some place where the boys think more of baseball and less of hell-raising." Persuasive arguments by Miller Huggins, who owned a winter home in St. Petersburg, Florida, and Albert Fielding Lang, former mayor of that city, convinced Ruppert to take his team to the Sunshine State. Yankees players and sports reporters who followed them were less than excited to hear that training would be in what they considered an old-folks town. Babe Ruth was heard to remark, "I wonder whether we can have any fun there."

As he got to know his teammates, Lou learned that baseball in the major leagues was different than at Hartford. And the Yankees were in a class all their own. They had a dreadful record in 1925, but they may well have had the most fun. Sportswriter Paul Gallico explained, "It isn't a game played for the sweet joy of sport by Sunday school book characters, but a rough, competitive game played as a profession and a business by a bunch of tough, hard-bitten men who were and are just like any other groups of men." He added that "they were the hardest drinking, hardest hitting ball club in the history of the game, the most colorful and the most exciting to watch." Gallico wrote that these Yankees were "grand and mad and wild, and goofy," but above all, they lived to "drink, wench, and clout the ball." Another writer from that period said, "Those Yanks never kept regular hours. They played bridge, stud, draw, blackjack, or red dog. They played the ponies, and they could make the night hideous on a Pullman with their singing and their horseplay." Lou did not fit in with this wild life, since he drank only an occasional beer, had no desire to go wenching, and always made curfew.

Babe Ruth, the worst violator of Huggins's code of conduct, took an interest in the young first baseman, "a young, sincere giant with a bow tie," in the words of Bob Considine. As for Lou, Paul Gallico recalled that he "sincerely adored Ruth, admired him, hero-worshipped him, and thought him a wonderful baseball player and an amusing man." At first, Babe took advantage of this fidelity to order the youngster to get things for him and fetch drinks and sandwiches. Later, Lou would act as intermediary between Babe and a slew of girls, telephoning them to arrange dates. Lou's wife would later recall, "The Babe's lusty love of life, his appetites, and his prowess with wine, women, and food was always a source of enormous amusement to Lou."

Babe would show his appreciation by offering Lou guidance. One day, in an unusually solemn tone, he gave Lou some good advice: "If a guy flops, if the managers turn against him, if everybody and everything goes back on a fellow, he can always be sure of his eats as a waiter. But Lou, a young fellow like you ought to save your money. Now, a bird has to think of the time when he can't play ball no longer." Ballplayers who overheard this recommendation howled with laughter. For years, they had watched as Babe threw away his money "with the casual, carefree air of a kid discarding peanut shells." In 1925 Babe confessed to having squandered $250,000 of his baseball and endorsement income. He did not want Lou to make the same mistake.

Babe Ruth and the Yankees had a terrible year in 1925. Babe showed up at the newly opened Crescent Lake Park overweight at 245 pounds and with another case of influenza. Having lost about fifteen pounds, Babe was starving and, at a whistle-stop, jumped off the train, where he "gluttonously gorged himself to the score of 12 hot dogs and eight bottles of poisonous soda pop." By the time he reached Asheville, North Carolina, Babe was understandably "green of face and filled with pain," suffering from acute indigestion, and withdrew from an exhibition game. Placed on an express train, Babe was rushed to New York, while word of his stomach ailment spread around the world. This affliction was compounded as the train approached Pennsylvania Station, when he fainted in his car's washroom and struck his head on the washbasin. He was rendered unconscious for about two hours, and the world held its breath while Babe recovered.

With Babe sidelined in the hospital by an abscess in his digestive tract, Lou filled the void. On April 11, he went in as a pinch hitter and smacked a ball over the left field wall at Ebbets Field in the Yankees' penultimate exhibition game against the Dodgers. The next day, the Yanks lost, making their preseason record against the Dodgers 10–7. Thereafter, their real season took a nosedive, and the New Yorkers finished in seventh place in the American League. Sportswriter Grantland Rice would explain that Lou Gehrig was one of the few bright spots that

year: "It gave him his first day-in-and-day-out experience playing with a big league club. It started him off on the most amazing
string of unbroken performances that any ballplayer, major or
minor leaguer, ever has given. And he closed it out hitting .295,
which wasn't bad for a busher and gave a promise—long since
fulfilled—of better years to come." So did his 20 home runs and
68 RBIs in three-quarters of a season.

On June 2, Wally Pipp remembered, "some lime blew into my
eye during the warm-up period, and the rubbing and all blinded
me so I couldn't play. Babe Ruth was always horsing around and
wanting to play first in exhibitions and such, but Hug was always
afraid he'd get hurt, and this day he told Gehrig to get in there
and see what he could do." That was all the excuse the manager
needed to bench the thirty-two-year-old Pipp, a lifetime .281
hitter whose batting average had plummeted. Lou had typically
shown up early and had coach Charley O'Leary hit grounders to
him for more than an hour. He then went to lie down in the clubhouse while the regular infielders practiced. Lou remembered
that day well: "While I was in the clubhouse, Miller Huggins
called me into his office and said, 'You go out there and play first
base today, and from now on.'" Astonished at his skipper's order,
Lou lay down to get as much rest as possible for his 1925 debut
at first base. His relaxation technique worked. Lou smacked a
double and two singles in five at bats.

While Gehrig may have been deficient at fielding and base
running, there was no doubting his power. One day a batting
practice pitcher sent a couple of fast balls right down the middle. Lou watched them pass, then stormed out to the mound,
bellowing, "Do you want to get killed? Pitch 'em away or close.

Never through the middle." The dumbfounded pitcher learned later that Gehrig's greatest fear was that he would someday kill a pitcher by hitting a massive shot back to the mound.

Gehrig, now styled "Custard Pie" in the press for his ability to swallow a piece in two to four bites depending on size, remained in the lineup, his place being cemented when luckless Wally Pipp was beaned in batting practice on July 2. A pitch thrown by a rookie named Charley Caldwell struck the left-handed hitter above his right ear. Pipp's concussion kept him on the bench for a month while Lou proved himself a capable replacement. A demoralized Pipp would confess, "At the end of that time, the job was so solidly his that I played only one inning at first base thereafter for the Yanks."

Lou Gehrig's 1925 season was filled with highs and lows, and the Yankees struggled to stay out of last place in the American League, finishing 69-85. Following the grim season, Miller Huggins told Ed Barrow that his men did not have the will to win. Barrow gave Hug permission to break up the team and find suitable replacements. Huggins booted four regulars and began to rebuild.

Spring training in 1926 started with two lopsided losses to the Braves, 18–2 and 16–4. The Yankees, described as "a rabble [that] clowned in witless confusion," seemed indifferent and their manager apathetic. Westbrook Pegler, one of the nation's most popular and influential writers, wrote a column that said, "Miller Huggins hasn't got a team to manage. And if he had one, he couldn't manage it." Ed Barrow sent a copy to Huggins and instructed, "Put this on the clubhouse bulletin board. Let those fellows see what one sportswriter thinks of them." Barrow was mad. Huggins was mad. The entire Yankees roster was mad. They concluded their preseason by beating the Dodgers fourteen games in a row, Lou batting over .400.

Gehrig's hitting did not let up. Four games into the regular season, on April 17, he stroked a single, triple, and home run in four at bats. Paul Gallico had seen enough to predict, "Gehrig's tremendous breadth of shoulders bespeak a long ride for the apple when he connects." Another writer prophesied that Lou "will make the Gotham fans rub their eyes." He continued, "Few players of recent years have shown so much improvement as Gehrig flashed in spring training this year."

Lou Gehrig's temper boiled over in a game against the Tigers on May 8. In the bottom half of the ninth inning, with the Yankees behind 7–5 and two outs, pitcher Earl Whitehill hit Lou's wrist with a curveball. Whitehill protested that the ball had actually nicked the knob of his bat. Umpire Bill Dineen was unsure and checked Lou's wrist before sending him on to first base. Earl walked over almost to Lou and began to call Gehrig "yellow" for squawking about being hit. An enraged Lou yelled back, "If you think I'm yellow, come under the stands," but moved to settle things then and there. Rookie umpire Bill McGowan grabbed Gehrig, while Dineen pushed Whitehill back to the mound. After Babe Ruth grounded out to end the game, Gehrig and Whitehill made faces at each other as they left the field, but cooler heads kept them apart.

Both teams entered the tunnel under the grandstand, where Lou confronted center fielder and manager Ty Cobb, screaming,

"You told Whitehill to hit me! He done it a-purpose! You're always picking on me ever since I been in baseball!" In the dim light of the tunnel, there ensued what became a full-on fight. It was Custard Pie Gehrig against Peaches Cobb, no holds barred. While either shifting to take another swing or being pulled off Cobb by Babe Ruth, Lou hit his head on a concrete pillar and fell stunned. Cobb jumped up and kicked at Babe and Lou with his spikes in the semidarkness, a flagrant violation of fighting rules. Only partially dressed, Babe chased Cobb into the Tigers' dressing room but was promptly thrown out, the door slamming behind him. Three months later, Custard Pie and Peaches were spotted on a ball field kidding around about rumors of hostility between them.

While his hitting sparkled, Lou still needed work on his fielding. Diligent practice paid off in spring training, when Marshall Hunt watched from the press box as Lou began "stopping any kind of batted ball and pulling from the dirt all the poor throws made by other fielders."

The 1926 Yankees squeaked by the Cleveland Indians to win the American League pennant with a 91–63 record. Lou put up a batting average of .313 with 47 doubles, 20 triples, 16 home runs, and 109 runs batted in, coming in tenth in the voting for Most Valuable Player. Miller Huggins's decision to choose Gehrig over Wally Pipp had paid off, as the latter, traded to the Cincinnati Reds in the off-season, hit .291 with 22 doubles, 15 triples, and 6 home runs. Both men were charged with 15 errors.

Great things were expected of Lou Gehrig and the Yankees when they played the St. Louis Cardinals in the World Series. Both let down the New York fans. The Yankees lost four games to three, the finale a 3–2 nail-biter in front of an embittered home crowd. Lou showed his lack of judgment on several occasions. He killed a rally in the second game when he was thrown out "by seven furlongs" attempting ill-advisedly to take third. In game three, Lou went for a grounder that should have been fielded by the second baseman, and an easy out became a base hit. In seven games, Lou went 8 for 23, averaging .348, but he scored only 1 run and knocked in just 3. He walked 5 times and struck out 4. It was an unhappy end to the 1926 season. The whole team would soon be redeemed.

Murderers' Row

The 1927 Yankees were not just good, they were damned over-poweringly good. During a Fourth of July doubleheader against the Washington Senators, Miller Huggins's squad displayed its newfound strength. The first game ended with New York on top 12–1, followed by a 22–1 drubbing in game two. As Senators first baseman Joe Judge left the field, he muttered, "Those fellows not only beat you, but they tear your heart out." In the two games, Lou went 4 for 7, with 2 home runs and 4 walks, while Babe went 5 for 7, with a triple and 3 walks. The Babe summed up the Yankees' power that season: "We never even worried five or six runs behind.... Wham! Wham! Wham! Wham! And wham! No matter who was pitching." Marty Appel, author of *Pinstripe Empire*, believes that the words "1927 New York Yankees" even today still "inspire awe."

Lou turned twenty-four during the legendary 1927 season and was one of the most eligible bachelors in the country. He was so famous that the United Press updated his statistics daily, along with the other "Big Five" of baseball: Ruth, Cobb, Speaker, and Hornsby. According to Waite Hoyt, "Gehrig was a smooth-faced Atlas, an all-American type, a typical first boy in the seat in Sunday school." Despite being young, good-looking, and educated, Lou was not particularly interested in women, although it was rumored he had dated one in Washington and another in Philadelphia. He received scores of mash notes from female fans but would just scan these "honeyed epistles" before tossing them into a wastebasket. Mark Koenig remarked slyly, "Although he had no trouble scoring while he was on the field, he had lots of difficulty doing so when he was *off* of it." Koenig continued, "He asked us to fix him up with a girl once and we demurred; we told him he wouldn't know what to do with one if we did."

Gehrig was devoted to his mother, baseball, and fishing. After a home game, Lou used to pick up Christina and head off to catch eels. Mom would pickle their catch and share it with the Yankees team, which came to believe that devouring the eels bestowed some sort of supernatural hitting power. Teammates never learned where Lou's fishing hole was located, only that it was "somewhere in the vicinity of Harlem."

When not on the baseball field or home with his family during the 1927 season, Lou took in a movie, went for a roller-coaster ride, or took long walks. He enjoyed keeping in shape, even spending five months working in a garage between seasons so he would not have to lose weight during spring training. Lou also skipped lunch to keep his weight in check.

Everyone liked Lou Gehrig. George Pipgras remembered, "There was no finer man that walked the Earth. He didn't drink, chew or smoke. And he was in bed by nine thirty or ten each night." Earle Combs used Lou's own personal measure of a man's worth, saying, "That Gehrig, there was a man, quiet and steady—a ballplayer's ballplayer." No one could turn Lou Gehrig, the mama's boy, into Babe Ruth the libidinous party animal, but the team did attempt to remake him into a newer version of the older slugger. After Lou joined the club full-time in 1925, some coaches advised the rookie to copy Babe's stance and swing. He tried for several weeks but admitted it was "a flat failure." Huggins saw a natural hitter being ruined and called off the experiment.

Lou's modesty would not allow him to assume much credit for his success at the plate. In the middle of his home run derby with Babe in 1927, Gehrig claimed, "My only thought is to drive in runs, for runs win ball games and victories win a pennant. I'll trade a single in the pinch where I have failed many times for one of my wasted home runs" that failed to achieve a Yankees win. Lou's success could be gauged by his amazing record of thirteen consecutive seasons of driving in more than one hundred runs. He modestly attributed his success to luck, stating one time, "It seems to me that it is all luck—just the luck of getting a ball from the pitchers you can hit at the time you are ready and set for it."

Lou led an interesting quartet of athletes in the infield. Tony Lazzeri, a card-carrying boilermaker in the off-season, brought along his nickname "Poosh-'Em-Up-Tony," earned in the minors during a slump when an Italian restaurant owner bought him plates of spaghetti and told him to "poosh 'em up." Tony had difficulty playing second base at Yankee Stadium and would later recall, "Many a time I've fielded a grounder, looked up, and couldn't see Gehrig fifty feet away on first base. Lou just merges into the background of the crowd, and you don't know whether you are throwing the ball to him or to a spectator."

Mark Koenig, a sandlot product of San Francisco like Lazzeri, and mysteriously referred to by the press as "Marcus Aurelius," arrived to play shortstop in 1925. Assigned the locker next to Babe and generally sleeping in a berth across from him on Pullman trips, Koenig fell in with the boozing boys. He quickly picked up some of the team's bad habits, remembering that on road trips, most men "carried an augur to drill through the walls to see what was going on in the next hotel room." He commented later, "It's a wonder they didn't get their eyes poked out." Koenig, a lover of dominoes and polka music, soon squabbled with Ruth. They wrestled a bit until the umpire threw both of them out of the game and did not make up until the Yanks won the pennant that year.

"Jumping Joe" Dugan was also part of Babe Ruth's roistering crowd that spent road trips drinking, gambling, betting on the ponies, and womanizing. Dugan "could drink quite a quantity and never show it." He also was an inveterate gambler; at the conclusion of each successful season, Dugan would squander his entire World Series check. On the diamond, Jumping Joe, like most Irishmen, was superstitious. He refused to ever throw a ball to the pitcher after a putout, fearing it would bring bad luck. One day the team exploded in a late-inning rally. Combs tripled, Koenig doubled, Ruth homered, Gehrig homered, Meusel doubled, Lazzeri tripled, Dugan singled. Afterward, Dugan was met by Huggins, who barked, "That'll cost you fifty bucks!" Dumbfounded, the third baseman asked why. The normally taciturn manager joked, "For breaking up a rally."

The Yankees' pitchers were a unique bunch. Right-hander Waite "Schoolboy" Hoyt, asked to reveal the secret to success for a major-league pitcher, replied simply, "Get a job on the Yankees." Shortly after Lou met Waite, the latter joined his father-in-law's undertaking business. One afternoon when he was scheduled to pitch, Hoyt received a telephone call asking him to pick up a corpse and bring it by at dinnertime. He drove over, stuffed the cadaver into his car trunk, parked at Yankee Stadium, pitched a winning game, and delivered his package in time for dinner.

Lefty Herb Pennock had the memory of an elephant and could help Yankees hitters correct their swings when in a slump. As for himself, it was said that Pennock "couldn't hit the water if he fell out of a canoe." His theory of pitching was simple: "Throw the batter off. Ruin his timing. Make him hit ahead of the ball, behind the ball, under it, or over it." Herb never swore or drank, always acting like a perfect gentleman, which led to his nickname the "Squire of Kennett Square." The thirty-three-year-old Pennock was a nervous sort, once confiding to third baseman Dugan during a tight situation, "Joe, I'm so scared, I can't even see the signs." Aware of Herb's excitable nature, Manager Huggins would never start Pennock in the first game of any road trip, since he could never sleep on trains.

George "Great Dane" Pipgras had joined the Yankees with speed and a good curveball but attributed his success to learning to control his pitches. During one game, he wheeled around and picked Ty Cobb off second base. Cobb responded with a torrent of expletives. To get even, during the Georgia Peach's next at bat, Pipgras said he intentionally threw two pitches "at the back of his neck." Cobb bunted the next delivery down the first base line and, as George picked up the ball, came at the pitcher feet first, inflicting scars that would last a lifetime. In the off-season, Pipgras earned $50 a day killing deer for wealthy Chicago sportsmen who could then brag about their trophies back home.

Veteran Urban Shocker, a perennial twenty-game winner for

the St. Louis Browns, began and ended his career in a Yankees uniform. A scientific pitcher, the five-foot-ten righty scoured newspapers for reports on batters as he sought an Achilles' heel to exploit. Despite his detailed studies of opponents, Urban was superstitious enough to never throw his glove on the grass of any ball field. Shocker began as an average right-hander, but his newspaper study and learning how to throw a good spitball added to his winning percentage. Spitballs had been banned league-wide beginning with the 1921 season, but Shocker had been grandfathered in and catcher Benny Bengough recalled that he, like the other spitball pitchers, "used to doctor the ball with so much saliva, you could see the spray when they threw it." Unbeknown to his 1927 teammates, Shocker had a bad heart and could sleep only by sitting up in bed.

The last important member of the Yankee pitching staff was a tall, raw-boned Oklahoma farmer named Wilcy "Cy" Moore. Joe Dugan joked that Moore was a mail-order right-handed pitcher because Ed Barrow had offered him a contract sight unseen. His most effective pitch was a sidearm sinker that broke down like a spitball, forcing batters to top the ball and hit into rally-killing double plays. One of the best relief pitchers in all of baseball, Moore would say modestly, "I ain't a pitcher, I'm a day laborer." Wilcy was such an abysmal hitter, however, that Babe taunted him and bet $15 at 20-to-1 odds that Cy would not get three hits all season. When Moore beat out an infield single on August 26, the slugger paid up. Wilcy used the money to purchase two mules for his farm, naturally naming them Babe and Ruth.

Bernard "Benny" Bengough came to the Yankees as a reserve catcher. Babe nicknamed him "Barney Google," after the popular google-eyed comic strip character, while Bengough would call Ruth "Jidge," as did everyone else on the team. This nickname was a colloquial version of George, although Babe insisted it was from "judge" due to his natural wisdom. When Babe gave Christina Gehrig a scrawny Chihuahua, she named it Jidge after him. For some unknown reason, Lou referred to Babe as "Jedge," a term usually reserved by ballplayers and writers for Judge Kenesaw Mountain Landis.

Bengough spent most of his time warming up relievers in the bullpen. Cut off from activity on the diamond, men in the bullpen told stories, laughed at jokes, ate ice cream, drank soda pop, played cards, and took naps. It was also a fine place to ignore the ballgame, as Benny explained: "They hear little and care less for the excitement, the howling, and the cheers as the baseball bugs in the stands go nutty over this home run or that shoestring catch." Bengough would confess, "I was the weak sister of the ball club. When I used to come up to the plate, after four or five guys ahead of me had hit homers, triples, and doubles, I used to say to the guy who was catching, 'Watch me stop this rally for you, kiddo,' and I usually kept my word."

With Benny Bengough recovering from an injury, Miller Huggins split catching duties between Pat Collins, monikered "Horse Nose," and John "Grabby" Grabowski. Pat, a smart receiver, made the pitcher appear to control the whole show. One of the Yankees' hurlers explained, "A catcher is the wife of the battery couple; he should humor the pitcher; give him cautious advice, build up the pitcher's pride and faith in himself, and take a backseat to the head of the family, and only do backseat driving when advisable." A good receiver and decent hitter, Pat's biggest drawback was that too often his throws to second base ended up in the glove of center fielder Earle Combs.

John Grabowski was described as a "weighty backstop." Other players noticed that he kept to himself and rarely asked for advice. Actually, he very seldom said anything, his fellow Yankees remarking that Johnny "doesn't speak twenty-five words in twenty-four hours, and these are spoken in passing the time of day or ordering his meals." Grabby chewed tobacco and could spit through his catcher's mask "with unerring accuracy." He thus became Urban Shocker's favorite battery mate, stealthily adding tobacco juice to his saliva-soaked spitball.

Yankees outfielders were an odd crew. "Long Bob" Meusel played left field primarily and was accurately described as "a lanky, silent guy with a rifle arm." Long Bob was even more incommunicado than Grabowski. Babe Ruth remembered, "I've seen Bob go through a whole day when I don't believe he spoke a word, unless it was at the dining table when he asked somebody to 'pass the bread.'" Ruth and Meusel were drinking buddies and could be found on off days in a New York brewery or at a Passaic, New Jersey, blind pig, where they quaffed beer and downed sandwiches in the illegal bar. On road trips, according to sportswriter Bill Corum, the pair's first response "in reaching their hotel room in any town was to peel down to the skin and order up a case of beer." On the homeward-bound leg of road trips, they would consume large amounts of beer and ribs, tossing bones and empty bottles at telephone poles along the tracks.

Center fielder Earle Combs came to the Yankees from the minor-league Louisville Colonels, so he was dubbed the "Kentucky Colonel." Earle was the complete opposite of Grabowski and Bob Meusel, never seeming to shut up. He was a notorious "barber," so called because men in that occupation constantly chatted with their customers. Combs never smoked or chewed tobacco, never played cards for money, and would not drink so much as a Coke. He was a good friend of Lou Gehrig's, both of them clean-livers and notorious penny-pinchers, so the two would often go see a movie together. Combs read the Bible in his hotel room and enjoyed playing golf. Perhaps his greatest contribution to the Yankees was to prolong Babe's career by catching long fly balls in what should have been right field territory, thereby saving Ruth's rickety legs.

Everyone in the country wanted to follow the exploits of America's Peter Pan, the man who never grew up. George Herman "Babe" Ruth knew his God-given talent was virtually limitless and attacked life as if it, too, had no boundaries. Placed in a Catholic orphanage by his mother and father, Ruth never learned the discipline that his parents had hoped the monks could give him. He joined the minor-league Baltimore Orioles at the age of nineteen but was quickly elevated to pitch for the Boston Red Sox. He soon turned into a Hall of Fame–caliber pitcher with a lifetime record of 94–46 with a 2.28 ERA. Ruth quickly developed into a power hitter and helped Boston win World Series titles in 1915, 1916, and 1918. Needing his hitting power more than his pitching, Boston management turned him into an outfielder and first baseman so he could be in the lineup every game.

With the Sox's owner in financial difficulty and the Yankees looking for a power hitter, the New York club purchased the rights to Babe Ruth for $100,000 so he could play in 1920. This deal would shape the Yankees franchise for years to come. Although known for his slugging ability in New York, he did pitch five games and won them all.

One writer summed up Babe's early attitude: "Easy living, easy money, easy women, easy booze." He chewed tobacco at the age of five and at ten was drinking beer, wine, and whiskey. By the time Ruth became a Yankee in 1920, he was fun to be around. Waite Hoyt recalled, "God, we liked that big son of a bitch. He was a constant source of joy." Mark Koenig said, "He was a big, overgrown kid, that's all he was," then added, "He was just interested in girls and drinking and eating." Ruth's first roommate in New York was veteran center fielder Ping Bodie. Asked whom he shared a room with, Ping responded, "Babe Ruth's suitcase." Earle Combs, who was not part of Babe's drinking crowd, had a different opinion of the famous slugger, declaring that "outside of baseball, he was as dumb as an ox."

Obviously, Ruth lacked formal education. Koenig noted, "I don't think he read any books. He didn't know the difference between Robin Hood and Cock Robin." Mark remembered that when a big crowd filled the stadium, Babe would comment, "Hey, the people are coming in groves." If there was not a cloud on the horizon, Babe would blurt out, "There's a vacancy in the sky today." A friend in the newspaper business explained that "he did not have to turn a page in a book or do sums in arithmetic to gain the knowledge he needed to become rich and famous." Ruth had a hard time remembering names and just called everybody "Kid."

Babe Ruth, like many ballplayers of his era, was superstitious. The Yankees team had its own good luck charm in Eddie Bennett, their "lucky hunch" and "midget mascot." Deformed by a spinal curvature in a childhood accident, Eddie came to the

Yankees in 1921 as a seventeen-year-old batboy and was soon elevated to team mascot and magical curiosity. Ruth, Gehrig, and Lazzeri always took their bats directly from Eddie. Pinch hitters always shook his hand before going to the plate. He would always greet every home run hitter as he scored. Herb Pennock stroked the hump on his back for luck. Once, during a team slump in 1922, Eddie came onto the field with his cap, stockings, uniform, and underwear turned inside out, an early version of the current rally cap.

In addition to being superstitious, Babe loved practical jokes. During the 1927 season, he was playing golf with Joe Dugan at a posh Westchester County club, driving well but putting dreadfully. He shouted, "Them damn squirrels running around are killing my game!" Babe sent his caddy off to procure a .22 rifle and finished the round taking potshots at squirrels, killing enough to stuff his face with potpie that night. In the clubhouse, he would occasionally nail a man's shoes to the floor or cut off the sleeves of his jersey. One of Babe's favorite jokes was to put a lighted cigarette into Tony Lazzeri's pants just before he pulled them up. Tony got even one day. His tormentor used to stuff a red handkerchief into his back pocket, which he would use to mop sweat from his face. Lazzeri set fire to the oversized hanky just as Babe started toward right field, streaming smoke and ashes as he swatted at the flames. Other teammates got back at Babe after an exhibition game in Minneapolis on July 20, 1927. Several players stopped by a local bordello, completed their business, and stole the madam's parrot. They hid their purloined bird in Babe's straw boater overnight in the Pullman car, so that he found his favorite hat torn to shreds and full of parrot poo.

Babe Ruth never had the physique of an athlete or the face of a movie star. He was homely by most standards, with a pug nose on a face too large for his body. His shoulders slouched, and his torso was barrel shaped, held up by scrawny legs that resulted in a goofy running style. One observer wrote, "He looked like a fat-bellied, beer-drinking guy who was 6'2", weighed 220, had skinny legs, and trim ankles like a girl." Another commented that those legs "were toothpicks attached to a piano." Babe smoked coffin nails and fat cigars. He was the titleholder when it came to belching and farting. His appetite for everything was prodigious, although he could usually confine himself to a "reasonable" six hot dogs and sodas. As for Babe's rumored consumption of beer and liquor, Hoyt came to his defense, saying, "Sure, he drank; most of us did. But he wasn't a drunk. And he never missed a game because of a hangover."

Despite being shaped like a barroom sot, by 1927, Babe Ruth had perfected the art of hitting home runs, having led the major leagues seven of the previous nine years. Ruth's highest total had come in 1921 when he hit fifty-nine four-baggers. He took up golf, thinking that swing would help his cut at a baseball. Practicing in his apartment was nixed after he'd broken a couple of his wife's expensive Chinese vases, but he learned to follow through like a golfer. Every muscle worked in sync, from his long arms to his pipe-stem legs. Mark Koenig said that Babe had a beautiful swing "even when he struck out." Herbie Pennock agreed, saying Ruth's swing was like "a circus with classical rhythm." Even when he did not connect solidly, good things could still happen. After the 1927 World Series, Babe Ruth admitted that he often judged a ball's trajectory, closed his eyes, and swung. He also confessed why he won the home run title that year with sixty: "I played for the ball club until we had the pennant won, and then I just concentrated on home runs. Anything that looked good, I swung at."

Babe Ruth and Lou Gehrig would lead their team into the 1927 season. Boasting what would be called "perhaps the most potent batting order the game has ever known," these Yankees were the first incarnation of the Bronx Bombers and, in the opinion of sportswriter Hall Brock, remain "baseball's measuring stick for offensive domination." But it was more than powerful hitters, good defense, and superb pitching, Lou explaining that the team's success was also built on the enigmatic impact of teamwork: "It's funny, but the minute you're up against a team with the will to win, you actually feel it. You can see it, too, if you watch closely enough. The men hustle. They back up plays. Every fellow goes out of his way to help the others, physically and morally."

That Storybook Season

Jacob Ruppert's fortune, combined with the baseball acumen of Ed Barrow and Miller Huggins, assembled what is arguably the best professional baseball team in history. The American author Damon Runyon referred to the process as "the strange human traffic of organized baseball in which men are bartered and sold in the marts of the game like cows, or pigs, or horses." Complicating their constructing the perfect team was the fact that baseball itself was changing. Until the 1920s, fans supported their favorite teams, but by 1927, newspaper reporters and radio announcers were emphasizing the accomplishments of individual players, and admirers began to follow emerging superstars. One writer explained, "A Ruth or a Gehrig is like a boxing champion, monopolizing all the ballyhoo."

With only slight modifications, Miller Huggins kept the same lineup except when injuries allowed reserve players to step up. Two college men, Joe Styborski of Penn State and Don Miller of Michigan, joined the club in June for tryouts and hung around long enough to appear in the team photograph before heading to the minors. His original roster never changed; no one on the team was released, and no minor leaguer got a chance to join the Yankees. It was a deadly arsenal of offensive power. Earle Combs led off, a good judge of pitches and a line drive hitter with the team's second-leading batting average, at .356. Mark Koenig batted second and was a dangerous switch-hitter. Babe Ruth filled the third slot and could hit with power to any field. He could also choke up to crack singles if necessary and was the best bunter on the team. Lou Gehrig batted cleanup and, like Ruth, could hit anywhere with power. His benefit to the team was obvious in the comment by umpire and columnist Billy Evans "It's like going from the frying pan into the fire when a pitcher gambles with Gehrig rather than Ruth."

Clam-silent Bob Meusel batted fifth, a "right-handed hitter who busted them a long way," and could be counted on for an average over .300. Tony Lazzeri, another .300 hitter, followed Meusel. A threat to either a left- or right-handed pitcher, Lazzeri used to swing for the fences at least one time in every at bat. This gave the Yankees four batters in a row who would drive in more than one hundred runs. Seventh in the lineup was Joe Dugan, a singles hitter whose job was to keep a rally going. Of the three catchers, Pat Collins and John Grabowski would always take healthy cuts but average only about .275. Benny Bengough saw limited action and batted .247. Pitchers always batted last. In April umpire Billy Evans summarized this Yankees lineup, declaring, "there is always danger in the air when the members of the Huggins troupe are in a hitting mood." Sportswriter Bill Corum said it perfectly: "Death, pestilence, and famine are nothing. When you really want to indicate complete devastation just say Ruth, Gehrig, and Meusel."

A rookie pitcher paid tribute to Lou Gehrig and his teammates on what the newspapers called "Murderers' Row." The novice hurler had just purchased a hot dog out in the bullpen when he was called to enter the game.

What's the situation? he asked. The answer came, "Three men on and nobody out."

Who's up next? he wanted to know. "Ruth, Gehrig, and Meusel." The rookie then announced, "Just save that hot dog for me. I'll be right back."

Although the term Murderers' Row has come to be associated with the 1927 Yankees, it predated this wrecking crew by almost a decade. The original version of Murderers' Row appeared in Yankees uniforms in 1918 and consisted of Roger Peckinpaugh, John "Home Run" Baker, Del Pratt, Wally Pipp, and Ping Bodie. The quintet banged all of 13 home runs—6 of them by Baker. By 1921, Murderers' Row included Ruth, Meusel, Aaron Ward, and Wally Pipp. In 1927 the label included the first six batters in the New York lineup. A nickname that actually began with the 1927 Yankees was "Five O'Clock Lightning." Earle Combs had gotten into the habit of checking his watch when the team began late-inning rallies. Since there were no night games then, with most contests beginning at three or shortly thereafter, these comebacks often occurred around five o'clock. One day as Ruth stepped to the plate with his team behind, Combs blurted out, "Five o'clock lightning!" Other players picked up the cry, and soon the league was buzzing. Rival pitchers heard the chant, columnist Frank Graham writing that "no matter how well they might be doing in the early innings, they dreaded the approach of the seventh inning . . . the eighth inning . . . the ninth."

Spring training in St. Petersburg began with unrestrained laughter and heckling when Babe Ruth arrived on March 19. Fresh from a stint acting in a Hollywood silent film, Babe made a flamboyant entrance attired in "mauve-tinted knickers, creased to a razor edge; cream-colored hose, banded in red; black-and-white shoes, blue belt, gray silk shirt, baby-blue tie, and to top it off, a creamy-white sweater with flaring collar." That was just too much even for other Yankees who sported silk shirts and ties and kangaroo leather shoes. Among those roaring the loudest at Babe's sartorial apparition was Lou Gehrig, who, according to his wife, always "got a kick out of his shenanigans," partly because he rarely bought new clothes himself and admitted, "I felt like a tramp," in comparison. Babe could give as well as take a joke, so later that year, he got back at Lou and his meaty torso when he told a reporter, "He came around here loaded to the decks with hog fat, and we took it off him. He still has some yet—above the neck—and we're workin' hard on that."

Babe's outrageous wardrobe was a mere distraction for Lou, who was ready to get into his daily spring training routine. Always conscious of his weight, he would don three sweatshirts and jog around the cinder track, with sweat pouring off him. Being especially concerned about his legs, Lou also put in untold miles on a stationary bicycle. He would later admit, "I try to keep the leg muscles limber. I stretch 'em every day for about five minutes. I think I'm good enough as far as the other muscles are concerned. But they say the legs go first, and I'm taking care of mine." On rare occasions, Gehrig asked the trainer for rubdowns, leaving the doc nothing more to do for him than place one stick of chewing gum atop Lou's locker before each contest. Following workouts and ballgames, he would sit in his sweaty clothes for as long as thirty minutes, sometimes smoking a pipe or cigarette and drinking a beer. It was Lou's way of relaxing his nerves and muscles before showering.

On opening day, April 12, seventy thousand spectators

jammed into Yankee Stadium to see their favorite power hitters vanquish the Athletics. The game proved disappointing despite being hyped in newspapers and radio broadcasts. Although the Yankees won 8–3, Gehrig only doubled in 4 at bats, while Ruth went 0 for 3 before being pulled for a pinch hitter. The following day, both players had 2 hits in 4 at bats, and on April 14 each went 1 for 3 in a game called after ten innings with the score tied 9–9. Ruth hit his first home run of 1927 into the right field bleachers on April 15, as the Yankees concluded a four-game sweep of Philadelphia. Two days later, Lou Gehrig finally exploded, slamming two rockets into the right field seats while driving in 6 runs and scoring 3 in a 14–2 romp over Boston. These mighty blows were the first shots in what would come to be called the home run derby of 1927, a term that would sell millions of newspapers as fans kept track of daily totals by Ruth and Gehrig.

Home run totals seesawed for most of the season. On May 16 against the Tigers, sportswriter Marshall Hunt wrote how Lou hit "a ponderous home run" into right field to tie Ruth with eight. A week later, both men hit solitary home runs that brought Ruth's total to eleven and Gehrig's to ten in a game lost to the Senators 3–2. Ruth pulled ahead by socking his twentieth on June 11 against the Indians, a game notable for Gehrig's being part of a successful double steal—quite an accomplishment, given his lack of base running skill. Gehrig began to come back on June 18, the day before his birthday, when he hit two against the St. Louis Browns. Following his sixteenth and seventeenth home runs, an admiring writer offered this comment: "Sturdy as an oak, this Henri [*sic*] Louis Gehrig, powerful legs supporting a robust body and huge arms rippling with their sinews." By the end of June, Babe and Lou, now dubbed the "Bust 'Em Boys," were tied with twenty-five apiece. Gehrig had surprised even Miller Huggins, who provided this assessment: "Somebody has given that bird more confidence than he ever had in his blooming life. It's grand to see that boy develop."

New York fans celebrated the Fourth of July with wins of 12–1 and 21–1 against the Senators. Lou belted a homer in each, bringing his season total to twenty-eight, now two ahead of Babe. But by July 9, Ruth was back on top with twenty-nine after hitting two against the Tigers. Gehrig leapfrogged into the lead by one when he homered twice against the Indians for numbers thirty-four and thirty-five. Both Yankees were tied after Ruth's thirty-ninth in an August 20 loss against Cleveland. Nine days later, Lou's forty-first against the Browns left him one behind his teammate.

Boston edged the Yankees 12–11 on September 5 in a game that ran eighteen innings, but Lou smacked his forty-fourth homer and again moved into a tie with Babe. The following day against the Red Sox, Lou busted another, but Babe came through with three, taking a lead of two. Then came what Lou termed "a bad slump," admitting, "I just couldn't get back into my stride." There was also a psychological component to the slump, and his mind seemed to be preoccupied. Christina Gehrig suffered from a large goiter that made it difficult for her to breathe and swallow, and doctors had advised Lou that she would require an operation. The twenty-four-year-old was also missing deadlines for his memoir for the *Oakland Tribune*. These pressures contributed to his not hitting another home run for more than three weeks. Newspapers noted the slump, with one upstate New York paper stating, "The home run pace of Babe Ruth has proved too fast for Lou Gehrig." A Brooklyn writer observed on September 14 that the Yankees had already won the pennant, leaving nothing of interest in the American League, then complained, "Even the home run race that Lou Gehrig made him stage is now a thing of the past; the Babe has practically mathematically eliminated Buster Lou."

Gehrig's next four-bagger would come on September 27, as well as a fifty-seventh for Ruth. Babe finished off his portion of the home run derby with two on September 29, to match his previous 1921 total, and number sixty came on September 30 against the Senators, leading one sportswriter to comment, "They could no more have stopped Babe Ruth from hitting that home run that gave him a new world's record than you could halt a locomotive by sticking your foot out."

Lou concluded his portion of the contest on October 1, the last game of the season, by driving the ball deep into the right field bleachers during the first inning. That day had been designated Gehrig Day. Before the first pitch, New York mayor Jimmy Walker presented Lou with an elegant wristwatch on behalf of the United German Society. Some thirty thousand spectators watched respectfully until Walker began to prattle; then impatient fans began to yell "Play ball!" and "We came to watch a ball game!" When action finally commenced, the Yankees beat the Senators 4–3 to finish the season 110-44—a .714 winning percentage. Once writers began to analyze the statistics, they realized that even though Babe smashed more home runs, Lou had accounted for thirty more total bases than his teammate by smacking more doubles and triples.

There were other noteworthy events besides the Ruth-Gehrig home run fest that year. Ford Motor Company began selling its Model A, with prices starting at $500. Al Jolson performed six songs in the landmark motion picture *The Jazz Singer*, ushering in the start of talkies. The Holland Tunnel opened to join New York City to New Jersey. Charles Lindbergh completed the first solo transatlantic flight, piloting the *Spirit of St. Louis* from Long Island to Paris. A celebration for Lucky Lindy was held at Yankee Stadium on June 16. Escorted by police motorcycles with screaming sirens, Lindbergh's limousine, several hours late, toured the outfield's cinder track before halting at the press box for photographs. A few salutes to the crowd, another turn around the outfield, and Lindbergh was gone.

On August 18 a report surfaced that Babe liked to snack on a pint of chocolate ice cream mixed with a quart of Mom Gehrig's pickled eels. Her recipe had become legendary. Inquisitive reporters finally convinced Lou's mom to give up her secrets: "Skin and clean the eels and let them stand in salt water for about 12 hours," she revealed. "Cut them into four-inch lengths, put into a stew pan, and cover well with a mixture half water and half vinegar, adding salt, pepper, bay leaves, cloves, and chopped onions. Cook eels in this for 15 minutes, covered. Take out the eels and let the gravy boil down. Put eels in a long pan, cover with the gravy, which will set into a jelly, and put away to cool." One sportswriter claimed that if Mrs. Gehrig would show up during the middle of a game with a bowl of her pickled eels, "that game would stop right there!" Christina explained why she cooked the slippery delicacy: "Lou has always been crazy about pickled eels. He'd rather have them than caviar. And he's always had all of them that he wanted." Apparently, Lou had more than his fill. When his future wife would ask if he missed this yummy treat, Lou, his preference now running to Cajun-style lobster, would blurt out "to keep the damned things off our table."

Mom Gehrig used to fix gargantuan dinners whenever Lou brought friends and teammates home. Some of the Yankees spent so much time in the Gehrig household they were like additional children, even calling her "Mom." Among Mom's favorites were Benny Bengough, Long Bob Meusel, Mark Koenig, and Babe.

Lou Gehrig was not the only Yankee to be honored with a special day. On September 1 a Brooklyn paper made the following announcement: "Da fans, dey planna beeg party for Tony Lazzeri nexa week opp in da balla park, watsa known as Yankee Stadioom. Da fans, dey say dees Tony Lazzeri the greatest balla player in da world so dey arrange a beeg celebrash." Translation: September 8 would be Tony Lazzeri Day. The reason was obvious to reporter Jimmy Wood, who wrote, "He has brought more sons of Sunny Italy to ball games who didn't know any more about baseball than I do about stroking a gondola." In typical fashion, Tony went 0 for 3 but drove in the winning run with a sacrifice fly, quite enough to keep a party going most of the night.

Earle Combs was recognized by a delegation from the dedicated center field crowd, who announced, "We've got a present for you, but we won't award it at home plate. It will have to be in the bleachers." Fans of the center fielder had chipped in pennies and nickels, collecting enough to buy him a $125 white gold watch. Two additional historic milestones were achieved on September 16, the day Lindbergh flew through in his fancy limousine. First of all, it was the team's one hundredth win, the first time the franchise had ever attained the century mark. Secondly, in perhaps the most remarkable thing ever seen by the 1927 team, pitcher Wilcy Moore, whose season batting average was .080, actually hit a home run.

The Yankees had torn through the American League like a tornado, leaving second-place Philadelphia a distant nineteen games back. One writer would say that the pennant race "might just as well have been a contest between a cheetah and a pack of snails." Their World Series opponents, the Pittsburgh Pirates, had muscled past the Cardinals and the Giants to finish first by a game and a half with a record of 94-60. Pirates manager Donie Bush ruled his team with an iron fist, fining and benching star outfielder and future Hall of Famer Kiki Cuyler in August after he failed to slide into second base, and never playing him again, despite a .309 batting average. His counterpart, Miller Huggins, had used a much less conspicuous way to handle Babe Ruth, his own personal prima donna. Cuyler would sit. Ruth would swing away. Neither team was familiar with the style or players of the other, so it would be a quick learning experience for both squads. Experts predicted that the Series would be a cliff-hanger pitting Pirates pitching against Yankees hitting, with victory possibly resulting from a bad hop, a wild throw, or an umpire's blown call.

All but five of the Yankees had postseason experience: pitchers Moore and Pipgras, catcher Grabowski, and utility men Julian Wera and Cedric Durst. Rain washed out much of practice at Forbes Field on October 3, although "Buster Gehrig flung his cap high in the air and did a dance today when he received a telegram that his mother had successfully undergone an operation for goiter." As part of his preparation on October 4, Lou explained:

"The day before the Series opened, I made a careful survey to see just how far I could go. I paced off the distance between first base and the nearest boxes at all angles and got a pretty good idea of how much room I had. Then I practiced running back without looking, and in a little while, I had those boxes so well placed in my mind that I didn't have to think about them anymore."

On the last day of practice, the Pirates finished up first, and many of them took seats to watch the Yankees take batting practice. Huggins put a carefully crafted plan into effect, telling Waite Hoyt to spend some time pitching for batting practice and "Just lay the ball in there." He sent fastballs down the center of the plate, and, as one observer would always remember, "up against the stands, into the stands, over the fences. It was a terrific demonstration of hitting power." Pirates players walked away shaking their heads, wondering how they could compete with such talent. They also had seen statistics that the New York club had belted 100 more home runs, 25 more triples, and 30 more doubles than Pittsburgh. The Series would come down to this: the Yankees' pitchers could allow their opponents to swing away, while the Pirates' hurlers could not afford to make that mistake. According to sportswriter Will Murphy, Huggins's men were a "sock-it-out-of-the-lot" team who could put up runs with just a couple of hits, whereas the Pirates were "a team of stabbing, jabbing, heckling, pesky tappers" who needed clusters of hits to score.

Waite Hoyt started game one against Ray Kremer. Everyone expected a sparkling pitching duel, but the Yankees won 5–4 in a sloppily played contest despite the Pirates outhitting the visitors 9–6. Wall Street brokers responded to the victory by offering

11-to-10 odds that the New Yorkers would win the second game in Pittsburgh and 2-to-1 odds they would take the fall classic.

October 6 began inauspiciously for the Yankees when Joe Dugan and Waite Hoyt announced that someone had broken into their hotel room while they were out partying and stolen several hundred dollars. Unfazed by this news, George Pipgras did a fine job in his debut against veteran righty Vic Aldridge. Young George went the distance and scattered seven hits over seven innings, "the hallmark of a boss pitcher." Big Apple sportswriters were not impressed with the National League opposition. The *Daily News'* Will Murphy wrote, "How a championship ball club can look so bad as the Pirates looked today remains one of the major mysteries of a confusing season. The Pirates not only *looked bad*, they *were* bad." Lou doubled and walked in four at bats, scoring one run in the 6–2 victory. Lou and Babe had yet to hit the ball out of the park, but it was noted that "Gehrig's fly in the fifth inning today sent Little [Paul] Waner out so far that the black paint of the centerfield fence showed on his shoulder blades." Odds on the New York team to win the third game, to be played at Yankee Stadium, remained at 11 to 10, but odds for them to win the Series were now 3 to 1.

Herb Pennock pitched a three-hitter in game three, an 8–1 cakewalk. Lou provided some of the excitement in the first inning when a titanic smash to deep center field drove in Combs and Koenig, but he was called out at home when he tried to stretch his mammoth triple into an inside-the-park homer. Babe contributed a home run in the seventh inning to deafening cheers from the stands. Summing up game three, a reporter for the *New York World* wrote, "The Pirates didn't look as if they could make a

run in a chiffon stocking." After the game, Lou walked up to Pennock and stared at his face. Confused, the southpaw asked what
he was doing. Lou responded, "Why, I heard some of the Pirates
say the other day that they would knock your ears off. I see they
didn't," then grinned so wide that his dimples looked to be six
inches deep. With the Yankees up three games to none, the *New
York Daily News* stopped printing odds.

Wilcy Moore started Saturday's game four. Taking the
mound in Yankee Stadium, he was "as calm and cool as though
he was pitching hay" back in Oklahoma. Moore hurled a complete game, although Gehrig provided no offensive help, going
hitless in five attempts. When he struck out with men on first and
third in the first inning, fans watched as Lou's temper flared, and
he "flung away his bat with venom." Babe hit his second homer in
two days during the fifth inning. Even Wilcy did better than Gehrig, the .080 hitter uncorking a single in the sixth. Earle Combs,
the next man up, screamed, "Run, run, Wilcy!" Moore, who
was said not to be on speaking terms with first base, supposedly
shouted back, "Which way?" This extraordinary event led writer
Will Murphy to comment, "Moore's base hit proves that we are
still living in the age of miracles."

Yankees fans "showed a goofy streak," cheering their team to
win the Series but also rooting for the Pirates because they wanted
to watch a Sunday game. Reserved seats for a possible fifth game
had already been sold weeks ago, and the money would have to
be refunded should the Yankees win. It was a strange situation
where the team would cost Jacob Ruppert's organization a great
deal of cash if it won. This made no difference to players who
would not receive any more compensation for prolonging the

Series past four games. So, with New Yorkers screaming in support of both teams, Huggins's squad filled the bases in the ninth inning of a 3–3 tie when Lou stepped to the plate with none out. It was his chance for a storybook ending to the World Series, but mighty Lou struck out. So did Long Bob Meusel. With Lazzeri at the plate, relief pitcher Johnny Miljus wound up and delivered a wild pitch to send Earle Combs racing in to seal the 1927 World Championship. Damon Runyon captured this anticlimax with a theatrical reference: "It was like getting all lathered up over a tense, nerve-wiggling, dramatic scene, and then having the low comedian step out and whack somebody over the noggin with a bladder."

Lou Gehrig had played a lackluster Series, garnering just 2 doubles, 2 triples, 3 walks, and 2 sacrifices in 18 trips to the plate, averaging .308 overall. The good news was that his fielding had been perfect, with 41 putouts and 3 assists. Better news was that his share of the World Series winnings came to $5,782.24. Lou's base running was best left unsaid. What's more, on October 11 the Baseball Writers' Association of America announced that Gehrig's lofty .373 average and 173 runs batted in, tops in all of baseball, had won him the coveted Most Valuable Player Award in the American League.

That winter, Lou negotiated a new contract with Jacob Ruppert for three years at triple his previous salary. He used the money to buy Heinrich and Christina a three-bedroom home at 309 Meadow Lane in New Rochelle, New York, taking over an existing $10,000 mortgage. He would live there with his parents until 1933, when he was thirty years old. Lou explained to a visitor, "It was a Christmas gift to my mother. I handed her the deed

Christmas day, though she knew I had my heart set on buying the place since last September when I first spotted it."

Everything was looking up for the Gehrig family. Lou had become a superstar, with money to match; Mom had a new home that her son was personally upgrading; and even Pop, now sixty-five, had resumed work as an iron mechanic in a business Lou had set up for him. As described in his memoir, Lou Gehrig, through persistence and natural ability, had achieved the American dream. But dreams do not last forever.

A Life Cut Short

Lou Gehrig had more than a decade's worth of highlights following the 1927 season, adding to his reputation as baseball's best first baseman. His home runs wouldn't stop. During a four-game World Series victory over the Cardinals in 1928, he hit four home runs and batted .545. On June 3, 1932, Lou belted four home runs in a single game, the first three off Philadelphia pitcher George Earnshaw. On August 17, 1933, in a contest against the St. Louis Browns, Lou set a new record for consecutive games played when he suited up for his 1,308th game, passing the previous mark held by his former Yankees teammate Deacon Scott. He downplayed the accomplishment, saying, "Why should there be so much fuss about a fellow sticking to a good, steady job? I can't see that's anything to get excited about. I like to play baseball, the Yankees seem to want me regularly on first base, so why not be in there right along?"

Twelve days later, Lou began another streak when he married Eleanor Twitchell, a Chicago society girl whom he had first encountered casually at a party in 1931. She changed his life, introducing him to travel, concerts, opera, and good books. Eleanor also cut Lou's ties to his mother's apron strings, and the pair enjoyed life as a couple without Christina overseeing his every move. A frequent visitor, writer Paul Gallico, would observe, "Lou, who had never known much gayety or frivolity, began to learn to enjoy life." He finally became comfortable around people, but away from the ball field, Lou preferred spending every minute with Eleanor. She learned to cook for him, but never the gargantuan meals his mother had prepared. For the first time in his life, Lou was truly happy.

Marriage seemed to agree with Gehrig, and in 1934 he won the American League Triple Crown with a batting average of .363, 49 home runs, and 165 runs batted in. These statistics came despite Lou's being beaned by a wild pitch in an exhibition game on June 29. Struck on the right temple, he lay unconscious for five minutes before Earle "Doc" Painter, who had succeeded Doc Woods as trainer, could revive him and send him off to be diagnosed with a concussion. This was after he had suffered a broken big toe on his right foot some ten days earlier. Lou won his second Most Valuable Player Award in 1936, ringing up 49 home runs and 152 runs batted in while hitting .354. In that year's World Series, Lou went 7 for 24 with a pair of home runs but was the goat when his appalling lack of skill on the bases cost the Yankees game five. Attempting to score from third, he hesitated for a second. One writer said, "He might as well have started for Des Moines," and he was called out at the plate.

After the Series, Christy Walsh, Lou's agent, convinced him to try Hollywood, where he sought to portray Tarzan in movies. Gehrig auditioned for the tree-swinging and lion-throttling role, but serious reporters lampooned the idea and referred to him as the MVP of the jungle. Hollywood was not interested.

Lou Gehrig marked an important milestone in his life on

March 23, 1938, when *Rawhide* premiered in St. Petersburg. Rebuffed in his attempt to star as Tarzan, Lou had signed on to play a cowboy in a film released by Twentieth Century-Fox. In one big barroom-brawl scene, Lou knocks out a gang of villains by throwing pool balls. The film's opening night included kleig lights, red carpets, traffic jams, and microphones to interview celebrity guests. Lou's cowboy performance was pronounced adequate, although he first had to practice riding on a pony equipped with handlebars. He was an easy target for jokes, one sports reporter joshing that the picture starred "Lou Gehrig and a horse who never played first base." One of his Yankees teammates declared that "Gehrig was far and away the best first baseman now in the movies." Lou was upbeat, declaring after the premiere, "I have everything a man could wish for: happiness and success. I've got the grandest girl in the world for a wife, wonderful parents, loyal and fine friends. I've just signed a good contract, and have money and securities in the bank. I'm on top of the world. Folks, I think I am the luckiest guy in the entire world." He would use these words again.

Lou had held out for more money in the spring of 1938, so he missed nearly all of training camp. Despite his cheery attitude, it was obvious even to casual observers that something was wrong. Doc Painter noticed that "he was underweight and couldn't seem to coordinate." Players joked that baseball and the bright lights of Hollywood did not mix. He could not hit pitches that would normally have been smashed to the fences, and it continued to get worse. By the first week in May, Gehrig had been demoted to batting sixth. Players talked among themselves and became divided on what to do, one group coming close to asking manager Joe McCarthy to remove their captain from the lineup. Although Gehrig seemed to come back somewhat later that season, finishing with 29 homers and 114 RBIs, his batting average slumped to .295—down nearly 60 points from the year before and the first time he landed below .300 since his first full season in 1925. After a liquor-infused celebration following the Yankees' four-game sweep of the Chicago Cubs in the fall classic, one shocked teammate, sensing something was definitely wrong, told Eleanor, "You better look out for Lou. He's drinking triples."

Despite an effort to get into tip-top shape, spring training in 1939 was even worse than the previous year. Doc Painter remembered, "I was standing by McCarthy when Lou took fielding practice for the first time. A grounder came along, and Lou reached and kind of tripped and almost fell down." Hall of Fame catcher Bill Dickey, Lou's longtime roommate, said, "He would stumble on the field making some easy play; for days he couldn't get a hit against the minor leaguers we played on the trip north." Reporters who had followed Gehrig's career for years were stunned at his performance, one of them admitting, "Judging strictly on appearance, Lou Gehrig is all washed up. He looks so bad, veteran newspapermen wonder whether he'll be able to last through the exhibition schedule." A survey of fifteen sportswriters disclosed that fourteen agreed Lou would be benched by fall. Lou and Eleanor rented an apartment away from the team, where he got secret leg massages and was measured for a special pair of spikes. None of it would help.

Doc Painter recalled, "It was pure torture for us that spring, and you know what it must have been for Lou. We knew he couldn't get out of his own way." Painter then admitted that "every time some wild young rookie wound up, I expected Lou to get it right in the eye. He could never have ducked one." Even Lou, now almost thirty-six, admitted things were not normal: "Right now, I can't get my bat around on the ball. Sometimes I can't even get my eyes focused on it as it comes up to the plate. But I know I'll be okay soon." But he never was okay, including off the field. Dickey explained that Lou had trouble even in a hotel room: "He started to take a little step forward to get something, and the foot he moved forward to start the step just didn't move right. Instead of swinging right out, it just moved a few inches in a faltering kind of way, and it threw Lou off balance, and he stumbled to the floor." Fred Lieb wrote that even Eleanor "began to observe that in stepping off the curb in crossing streets, Lou stepped down like a blind man. His foot would plop down on the concrete, as though he hadn't noticed he had reached the curb." Joe McCarthy, who loved Lou like a son, summed up the situation best: "If he were a rookie, we wouldn't carry him."

Gehrig's 1939 season was a disaster. After eight games, Lou had four hits in twenty-eight at bats for a batting average of .143. He would confess later to Grantland Rice, "I knew something was far wrong, but I had no idea what it was. Even when I met the ball squarely, a child could have hit it harder." After a home stand against the Senators, the Yankees headed to Detroit for a couple of games. Unknown to anyone else besides Eleanor, Lou had resolved to end his streak of 2,130 continuous games, after teammates had gone overboard in congratulating him on a routine play. He would later admit, "They meant it to be kind, but it hurt worse than any bawling out I ever received in baseball. They were saying 'Great stop!' because I had fielded a grounder. I decided then and there, I would ask McCarthy to take me out of the lineup." A further push for him to retire came from the home crowd that rained down boos, jeers, and catcalls when he failed to drive in runs after having three chances. A Brooklyn paper said simply, and cruelly, "Gehrig is dead wood."

When Lou limped to home plate with the lineup card on May 2, there was a smattering of applause from the confused Tigers fans. Then came an announcement over the public address system that Gehrig would not be starting. Joe McCarthy recalled, "The fans broke out in the biggest ovation I have ever heard. They cheered, stomped their feet, and whistled for fully ten minutes. Lou just stood there, head bowed, shaken by the tribute. There wasn't a player in the Yankee dugout whose eyes were dry. As Lou walked slowly back, we could see that he, too, had tears in his eyes." It was an incredible show of affection from a crowd that had rooted against Lou Gehrig and his Yankees for years.

Thus, the April 30 home contest against Washington would turn out to be Gehrig's last major-league game; his new duties consisted of cheering on the team and taking the lineup card to the umpires before each game. Following a doubleheader against the St. Louis Browns on June 11, the Yankees played an exhibition game against the Kansas City Blues of the American Association the next day. Lou went three innings and hit a feeble grounder in his only at bat. On June 12, McCarthy and the Yankees entrained for New York City while Lou headed to Rochester, Minnesota, for a thorough checkup at the Mayo Clinic.

Gehrig was examined by a team of doctors from June 13 to 19, although there were periods of relaxation and fun. Lou reminisced and clowned around at the nearby butcher shop of Julian Wera, a utility player on the 1927 Yankees. On his weekend off, he and one of his doctors cruised the Mississippi River. Mayo employees celebrated Lou's thirty-sixth birthday with an impromptu party at his hotel. But all amusement ended with the medical conclusion that Lou was suffering from amyotrophic lateral sclerosis, a wasting neurological disease with no known cure. His baseball career was over. There were no prescriptions, only a list of exercises and a series of spinal injections of vitamins B1 and B2. This deadly disease would quickly be referred to as either ALS or Lou Gehrig's Disease.

Lou Gehrig remained confident that he would beat this affliction the same way he had overcome every obstacle in his life. At least he now knew what he faced. Grantland Rice remembered Lou telling him, "The other night, I was pouring coffee for some guests and had to quit at the fourth cup. But some way or another, we'll find our way, and I'm too glad to be out of that terrible fog to bother too much about the rest." Even after his diagnosis, Doc Painter declared, "He was the most cheerful guy you ever saw." But his physical slide continued unabated. Painter had given Lou a single stick of gum before every game, but now something was different: "He'd thank me, but he'd just stand there and hold it. I realized he couldn't even take the paper off. After that, I was careful to peel it for him, but I never let on that I noticed."

To recognize his contributions to the Yankees and major-league baseball in general, the club proclaimed July 4, 1939, Lou Gehrig Appreciation Day. Celebrated journalist Bob Considine wrote with no exaggeration, "Baseball reached the most dra-

matic moment of its lifetime yesterday afternoon at the Yankee
Stadium." Before the first game of that day's doubleheader, Lou
met with more than a dozen veterans with whom he had shared
a locker room. A good chunk of the 1927 Yankees had arrived to
reminisce, laugh, and tell the same old lies about the time they
had ruled baseball. Even Babe Ruth showed up, albeit late as
usual. Lou enjoyed this reunion immensely but did apologize for
not remembering to order a keg of beer.

The old timers took their seats in the stands to watch the
first game, while Lou and a few friends sat in the shady Yankee
dugout. His old friend Considine sat next to what one reporter
called this "wasted ghost" until Lou was introduced over the
loudspeakers. Considine reminisced about what happened then:
"He picked up his cap and stood up. And then, out of sight of the
crowd, he toppled over backwards in a spell of helpless weakness.
I helped catch this uncomplaining, stout-hearted shell of what
had been the strongest athlete I ever knew. He said he was sorry,
and walked slowly out to home plate for the last time in his life."
He did not want to talk to the crowd, but after receiving several
armloads of gifts, Lou had no choice. Eager fans began to chant,
"We want Lou!" so he carefully shuffled to the microphone and
began to speak from the depths of his soul.

"Fans, for the past two weeks, you have been reading about a
bad break I got. Yet today I consider myself the luckiest man on
the face of the earth. I have been in ballparks for seventeen years,
and have never received anything but kindness and encouragement from you fans. Look at these grand men. Which of you
wouldn't consider it the highlight of his career just to associate

with them for even one day? . . . I might have had a tough break; but I have an awful lot to live for."

There were few dry eyes among the more than sixty thousand fans, the invited guests, and hundreds of thousands of radio listeners. Considine wrote, "This was Gehrig's last great moment in a sport that will never forget his name." His old pal Tony Lazzeri, speaking for all the veterans, would admit, "I thought I was all through crying when I was a kid, but that was before this afternoon." In typical Gehrig fashion, Lou wiped tears from his eyes as he stumbled back to the dugout, where he asked a close friend, "Did my speech sound silly? Did it?"

Although he never played in another game, Lou continued to collect a Yankees paycheck until the season's end, then was voted a full share after the team swept Cincinnati in the 1939 World Series. In a special election held on December 7, he was voted into the Baseball Hall of Fame in Cooperstown, New York, where he would be later joined by other contemporaries such as teammate Babe Ruth, nemesis-turned-friend Ty Cobb, and his idol Tris Speaker. Lou wanted to stay with the Yankees in some capacity but declared firmly, "I don't want any sympathy." He explained to Bob Considine: "If I wanted sympathy for this thing that's hit me, I'd have taken the lineup up to the plate every day during the World Series, and the fans would have given me a lot of applause. I know they would, but that's not what I want. I love baseball, and I think there must be some kind of job in it for me. If it only pays twenty-five bucks a week, I'll take it, but it has to be a job that I can honestly fill, a job I can say is my own—not something created for me." Plans for Lou to become a radio announcer fell through, and he spurned an outrageous sum of money to act as a greeter at a New York nightclub. Pride would play a big role in his choice of a new occupation.

A reasonable job proposal came in 1940 when Mayor Fiorello La Guardia of New York City offered a ten-year appointment to the city's Parole Commission. Lou accepted the offer, saying, "I am through with baseball and have severed my connections with the Yankee club. I may organize some baseball teams among prison inmates later—we'll see." The opportunity offered by sports had been brought into sharp focus several years earlier when the Yankees had played an exhibition game at Sing Sing Prison, and Lou had been greeted by several convicts—kids he had played with in his old neighborhood. He enjoyed his work immensely, claiming that "sports seem to give you the horse sense, the sense of justice, and, I guess you'd call it, fair play that the parole job demands." Lou tried to impress upon parole applicants that sports could change their lives "spiritually and mentally and physically." He said, "I keep telling those paroled men to go to a YMCA at night and work out, instead of to a corner saloon. I tell them to read, too . . . to do anything that will keep their mind in the right channel."

Ed Barrow devised suitable tributes. On January 6, 1940, he announced that Lou's number 4 would be retired so that no other Yankee would ever wear it—the first time in major-league baseball that an individual had been so honored. He also decreed that Lou's old locker would be reserved for his personal use, with "Gehrig" to remain in chalk; no one else could ever use that hallowed space. In addition, Barrow declared that Lou would be placed on a voluntary retired list so that he would technically remain a Yankee forever, with the freedom to come and go in the locker room.

Lou retained his interest in baseball, taking in about a dozen games during 1940. He came late to the ballpark in civilian clothes, entered a back entrance, sat unobtrusively in the Yankees dugout, and left before the game ended. His movements were slow and uncertain, so he tried to avoid getting in anyone's way or eliciting any sympathy. Babe Dahlgren, who had replaced Lou at first base, said sadly, "I handed him a cigarette. He could handle it, but I had to light it for him." Another man noted, "He was a hopeless figure on those brief occasions when he came to Yankee Stadium, stumbling around underneath the giant stands where he had thrilled numberless thousands with his mighty home runs. It made you choke up just to see him."

By the end of 1940, Lou was sleeping more, usually in bed by nine o'clock and up shortly after seven next morning, with a nap before dinner after feeding peanuts to pheasants who roamed the yard. He had lost weight, pointing to his stomach and telling visitors with a laugh, "I'm developing a pouch." The disease began by stealing his leg muscles, spread to his arms, and then "his face started to wither away." A strange pallor crept over his countenance, and that immaculate hair began to turn gray. When he could no longer go to his office, his wife and his close friends kept his true condition from the public. He and Eleanor would forego any social life to stay home, read, and listen to the radio. Christy Walsh dropped by and was shocked that Lou could not strike a match or write more than a couple of words. Eleanor confessed years later that "he never gained, just died away by inches, every day a little bit more, and if you saw him at the end of a week, you couldn't remember what he had looked like at the beginning of the week."

Eleanor was living a nightmare: "As the disease progressed, he couldn't dress himself, he couldn't feed himself, he couldn't walk." She hired a male nurse to dress and undress her husband. His wife would say sadly, "To watch someone close to you become a helpless, hopeless paralytic and to know that medical science is powerless to halt the progress of the disease is something no person should be called upon to endure." With his mind still active as ever, Lou Gehrig found himself trapped inside a body he could no longer control. The only blessing was that he was never in pain. Ed Barrow, one of Lou's last visitors, told how he never gave up: "When I left him the last time Friday night, he was sitting up looking out serenely across the Hudson. I kissed him on the head, and as I walked out, he said: 'I'll beat it, boss.'"

Lou Gehrig died peacefully at 10:10 p.m. on June 2, 1941, in his home at 5204 Delafield Avenue in the Bronx. The next day, as accolades poured in from celebrities and former teammates, fans began to queue up for the official two-hour viewing at Christ Episcopal Church, just around the corner from Lou's home. Five thousand fans stood in line to walk past Lou's open casket. There were taxi drivers, professional men, laborers with greasy hands, young boys, artists, reporters—every sort of person who had gone through the turnstiles at Yankee Stadium to watch Lou Gehrig play or had listened as radio broadcasters chronicled his latest home run. A funeral service took place on June 4 for one hundred invited guests.

One man who stood in this stream of humanity described his

experience: "You moved along a flagstone walk between lines of policemen to the steps of the church. A red-haired boy in a dirty sweatshirt, a baseball cap in his hands, was just ahead of you. Behind you there was a blind man, touching the arm of a younger man for guidance. The sun was reflected by his white cane." A policeman made sure everyone entered in a single file. The mourner picked up his narrative:

"Soon you were looking down at the calm face of one of baseball's immortals. He lay in a plain, dark casket, a blanket of roses covering his lower half. In a moment, you were past, moving on to the side door of the church. Behind you, you could hear the blind man whisper: 'Good-bye, Lou.'"

Fading into History

Yankee players acted quickly and contributed to a fund for a memorial to their old friend, which was dedicated on July 6, 1941. Beneath an image of Lou on the bronze plaque were heartfelt words composed by the ballplayers:

June 19, 1903—Henry Louis Gehrig—June 2, 1941

A Man, A Gentleman, and A Great Ball Player.

Whose amazing record of 2,130 consecutive games
should stand for all time.

This memorial is a tribute from the Yankee players
to their beloved captain and former teammate.

Venerable Connie Mack, part owner and manager of the Philadelphia Athletics, delivered a brief speech that included the following observation: "Lou Gehrig's conduct on and off the field was that of a gentleman and a sportsman. I am asking you to follow in the footsteps of our beloved friend." The memorial stood in center field, actually in the field of play, beside one erected to Miller Huggins following his death in 1929, and is now located in the new Yankee Stadium's Monument Park, behind the center field wall. After Lou Gehrig was cremated, his ashes were placed temporarily in the family vault of Ed Barrow in Kensico Cemetery, located in the aptly named Valhalla, New York. When a suitable monument had been installed in the nearby Gehrig plot, a bronze box containing Lou's remains was carried to their final resting place on September 13, escorted by Eleanor, his parents, Christy Walsh, and a dozen close friends. This same crowd would gather again on April 29, 1942, to unveil two memorial plaques to mark Lou Gehrig Plaza at 161st Street and the Grand Concourse in the Bronx. Visitors still visit Lou's grave in Kensico Cemetery, leaving mementos such as ball caps, baseballs, and even a license plate bearing the number 2130.

Lou's father was the first to follow Lou to the grave. Heinrich and Christina had become naturalized American citizens in 1944, and he died on August 16, 1946, at Harlem Valley State Hospital, an institution for the insane. Having lost the house that Lou had bought her when the mortgage holder foreclosed in 1937, Christina moved in with friends in Milford, Connecticut, dying in the local hospital on March 10, 1954, following a stroke. She was a great supporter of Little League Baseball, often sitting through long doubleheaders. Eleanor died March 6, 1984, at Presbyterian Hospital in New York City after being ill for about seven months. She had faithfully attended Old-Timers' Day and any World Series games played at Yankee Stadium, generally sitting next to Babe Ruth's widow, Claire, the Bambino's second wife. She attended the 1983 Old-Timers' Day game and ceremony in a wheelchair and, when introduced to the crowd, received a sincere greeting from the fans. Her will donated money to fund the Eleanor and Lou Gehrig Foundation to help find a cure and treatment for amyotrophic lateral sclerosis. Eleanor and Lou had no children.

As the 1941 World Series between the Yankees and the Brooklyn Dodgers approached, both teams agreed that a tribute to Lou Gehrig should appear on the official program. A portion of that testimonial read: "Natural strength, acquired skill, tireless industry, and unswerving loyalty brought Lou Gehrig to the top in baseball, the Iron Man of a great era in baseball history. He was the idol of the fans and the finest fellow in the world to those who knew him best—the players—competitors as well as team-mates." Their encomium continued: "This Yankee team couldn't go into another World Series without thinking of Lou Gehrig who led them to so many triumphs in the past. Nor could the fans of New York or Brooklyn forget his character, his modesty, his accomplishments—they will stand out in the recollections of all who follow sport in the years to come."

Gehrig had predicted a war with Germany as far back as 1935. Bill Dickey remembered, "He'd complain that we ought to start preparing for it. Sometimes the other players would kid him about it, and tell him nothing could ever happen to the United States, and that we'd never have to go to war again." Lou especially hated the German American Bund, organizations of pro-Nazi American citizens. He told Dickey, "I would like to go up there with a baseball bat and break up one of those little get-togethers all by myself. I would smack some of those skulls a lot harder than I ever hit a baseball."

Indeed, war came to America at Pearl Harbor on December 7, 1941, and Lou Gehrig's name became an important part in keeping the country fighting. On January 26, 1942, a charity drive commenced to purchase a fleet of vehicles under the auspices of the British American Ambulance Corps, each to carry an inscription that read "4—Lou Gehrig. Given by his friends to the City of New York, 1942," 4, of course, being his uniform number. Two years later, students from the High School of Commerce raised enough money to purchase an ambulance in memory of their honored graduate, this transport bearing the name "The Spirit of Lou Gehrig."

Interest in Lou ran high as the war rolled on. Foster Field, a fighter pilot training school in Texas, named its athletic field after him. When Fred Lieb wrote an article titled "Life of Lou Gehrig" in the 1942 issue of *Baseball Register*, one copy found its way to Morrison Field, United States Army Air Transport Command, outside of West Palm Beach, Florida. The lucky owner would explain, in the words of Hugh Fullerton, that "there are about 50 soldiers from the Bronx and Brooklyn in his barracks and he has a waiting list a foot long of fellows who want to read the Lou Gehrig biography in his copy of the *Baseball Register*."

More recognition of Lou was about to burst. Film producer Samuel Goldwyn began filming the movie *The Pride of the Yankees* on February 2, 1942, the screenplay written by Lou's old friend Paul Gallico with cooperation from Eleanor Gehrig. After considering a number of Hollywood stars, Goldwyn signed Gary Cooper to portray Lou for $150,000. He would explain his motivation for backing the film: "The one thing that moved me to make this picture was the story of Lou Gehrig, the man. It is one of the most inspiring and, at the same time, tragic stories I have ever known." Goldwyn continued, "Baseball is simply the backdrop for this story, which is, in a broad sense, the story of the opportunities that America offers every boy and of the whims with which life sometimes favors a few and then destroys them."

Cooper was an ideal choice to play Lou Gehrig. A major movie star, he had established himself by portrayals of the common man in *The Virginian*, *A Farewell to Arms*, and *Sergeant York*. Bearing a resemblance to Lou, his screen depictions appealed to both men and women. He accepted the role only after Eleanor thought he would be perfect to portray Lou. *The Pride of the Yankees* film would become one of 1942's top grossing films and would be nominated for eleven Academy Awards.

At the premiere in the New York metropolitan area, more than a hundred thousand moviegoers crammed into forty theaters to see what one reviewer called "a warm and gentle drama about a man whose life was lived in warmth and gentleness." Unknown to viewers, Gary Cooper knew no more about playing baseball than Lou Gehrig had known about riding a horse. Furthermore, the actor was right-handed; Gehrig, of course, swung from the left side. Hollywood took care of that potential problem by having Cooper wear a backward number 4 on his Yankees jersey and then flipping the film so that he appeared to be a lefty hitter like Lou. One unique aspect of this Twentieth Century-Fox film was that four characters were played by themselves instead of actors: Babe Ruth, Long Bob Meusel, Marcus Aurelius Koenig, and Bill Dickey, Lou's last roommate. Meusel was cast perfectly—he had no lines.

While the film neared completion, Samuel Goldwyn chanced to meet Damon Runyon and asked, "Why don't you write the foreword to my Lou Gehrig picture?"

Runyon responded, "I'll be glad to do so, and for free." Every program would contain these words of Runyon's:

> *This is the story of a hero of the peaceful paths of everyday life.*
>
> *It is the story of a gentle young man who in the full flower of his great fame was a lesson in simplicity and modesty to the youth of America.*
>
> *He faced death with that same valor and fortitude that is now being displayed by thousands of young Americans on far-flung fields of battle.*
>
> *He left behind him a memory of courage and devotion that will ever be an inspiration to all men.*

After watching *The Pride of the Yankees* at an improvised theater with seats made from discarded oil drums, gas cans, and old boxes, one soldier wrote to Eleanor from Libya: "Even though Lou is not over here fighting with us, his spirit and courage did much to instill in us the desire to continue this battle to keep alive the things people like you and Lou stand for—and what America stands for. He certainly hit a home run into our hearts."

Lou Gehrig's name continued to contribute to the war effort. The SS *Lou Gehrig*, a 10,500-ton Liberty ship, slipped into the water at South Portland, Maine, on January 17, 1943, after his mother christened the vessel. Children from Lake Pleasant Central Rural School in upstate New York had won the privilege of naming the ship by collecting nearly 120 tons of scrap during a state salvage drive. The SS *Lou Gehrig* was the first Liberty ship to be named after a famous athlete, beating out other New York notables such as Theodore Roosevelt and De Witt Clinton. When the ship was empty, its armed guard would play softball in the number two hold. Lou would have been proud of that. Used primarily on the Atlantic run, the SS *Lou Gehrig* landed 480 soldiers and 120 vehicles at Normandy June 19, 1944, on what would have been Lou's forty-first birthday. This was in support of the D-Day invasion that would eventually liberate France and defeat the Nazi war machine.

Gehrig's popularity, even after death, was not confined to New York. A staff sergeant from Idaho would write, "I think Lou Gehrig was the greatest athlete that ever lived. He stayed with his line longer than any other player and was faithful to his club until his very last game. To me he personified the typical American athlete." A Minnesota private would add, "Lou Gehrig is the greatest all-around athlete. He was a great football player in his college days, and certainly was the greatest baseball player that I know of. Besides all that, he was a real man. His achievements will stand for many years to come."

Fans showed how deeply rooted their admiration for Lou Gehrig remained during the Fourth War Loan Drive. Votes were cast by buying $25 series E war bonds—initial cost, $18.75. Gehrig led the voting from the start and amassed a total of more than $386,000, including a purchase of $8,000 by Bill Dickey. But he was edged out by New York Giants slugger Mel Ott, also the team's manager, whose fans came forth with a flood of purchases on the final day. However, the greatest show of support for Lou's memory came in Dallas on June 21, 1944. Eleanor had sent Lou's 1934 MVP trophy to her brother with the simple note "This may save a life." Frank Twitchell Jr., then serving in the US Army Air Forces, offered the prized possession to a war bond auction, where it brought a cool $1 million in bonds before being deposited at McCloskey General Hospital.

While Lou Gehrig's name had helped to win World War II, many people could not accept the fact that they would never see him again. Whitney Martin, a sportswriter for the Associated Press, wrote, "He's gone, but to the millions who saw him, he's as fresh in the memory as yesterday. The true Yankee fan never will go to the vast grey stadium without half expecting to see old piano legs jog out to take his stand at first base, his easy carriage and massive frame symbolizing more than anything else the confidence and power of the champions." Syndicated columnist George Matthew Adams penned his own memorial to Lou: "The love that people had for this man was sincere and deep buried. . . . Yes, we all knew him. Even those of us who never met or talked with him. We saw him in action. We read of his unique triumphs, gloried in his fame, and were thrilled by his matchless simplicity and modesty in the face of cheers for him that rocked many a great stadium."

Perhaps sportswriter Fred Lieb, Gehrig's friend, said it best when he wrote that "born under the shadow of the Statue of Liberty, breathing the early clean air of freedom, inculcated with the spirit of fair play in American scholastic and collegiate sports, he developed into a fine upstanding American, one of the nation's peacetime heroes, whose life already has served as an inspiration for millions of American boys." Jack Smith's sports column in the *New York Daily News* contained a unique, yet fitting, quotation after Lou took himself out of the lineup. It was from Shakespeare's *Julius Caesar*, act 5, scene 5:

> *His life was gentle, and the elements*
> *So mixed in him, that Nature might stand up*
> *And say to all the world, "This was a man!"*

Some newspapermen recycled Vice President Thomas Marshall's comment upon the death of Theodore Roosevelt in 1919 because it so aptly summarized Lou Gehrig's character up to his very last day: "Death had to take him sleeping; for if he had been awake, there would have been a fight!"

Over his lifetime, Lou Gehrig had won countless honors, gifts, medals, titles, prizes, ribbons, memorials, and accolades. His baseball achievements literally stuffed the record books. Writers competed against one another in an attempt to capture the essence of the man during his lifetime and after his death. Though Lou was held in great esteem by everyone who knew him, most commentators overlooked the most important part of his life. No longer able to play baseball, Lou threw himself wholeheartedly into a new career devoted to the young men of New York. His final days were spent encouraging them to change their lives and transcend their bleak surroundings through sports, all done without headlines, fanfare, or public recognition. Even when he could barely sit in his office chair, Lou came to work every day. There is no telling how many lives he changed in his time with the Parole Board, but every teenager he talked with had his undivided attention. Even as he slipped away as his disease progressed, Lou realized that every life was precious and worth saving. He had become an inspiration to young men and kids all over New York City. That is why hundreds of them came by subway and bus to file past his coffin, many with dirty jerseys, baseball caps askew, and holding worn ball gloves. These youngsters were the real legacy of Lou Gehrig.

Roster

This list provides brief descriptions for the careers of the many players in Lou's narrative who are now largely unknown. These sketches do not extend beyond 1927, the year *Following the Babe* came out, reflecting Lou's knowledge at that time. Careers do not include stints with minor-league clubs. Players who have been inducted into the Baseball Hall of Fame are indicated by a bullet (•).

Aldridge, Victor Eddington "Vic"—right-handed pitcher, Chicago Cubs, 1917–23; Pittsburgh Pirates, 1924–27

• Barrow, Edward Grant—manager, Detroit Tigers, 1903–04; Boston Red Sox, 1918–20; general manager, New York Yankees, 1921–27

Barry, John Joseph "Jack"—infielder, Philadelphia Athletics, 1908–15; Boston Red Sox, 1915–19; manager, Boston Red Sox, 1917

Beall, Walter Esau—right-handed pitcher, New York Yankees, 1924–27

Bengough, Bernard Oliver "Benny"—catcher, New York Yankees, 1923–27

Benton, Lawrence James—right-handed pitcher, Boston Braves, 1923–27; New York Giants, 1927

Berg, Morris "Moe"—infielder, Brooklyn Robins,* 1923; Chicago
　　White Sox, 1926–27

Buckeye, Garland Maires "Gob"—left-handed pitcher, Washington
　　Senators, 1918; Cleveland Indians, 1925–27

Burns, George Joseph—outfielder, New York Giants, 1911–21;
　　Cincinnati Reds, 1922–24; Philadelphia Phillies, 1925

Bush, Leslie Ambrose "Bullet Joe"—right-handed pitcher, Philadelphia
　　Athletics, 1912–17; Boston Red Sox, 1918–21; New York
　　Yankees, 1922–24; St. Louis Browns, 1925; Washington Senators,
　　1926; Pittsburgh Pirates, 1926–27; New York Giants, 1927

Bush, Owen Joseph "Donie"—shortstop, Detroit Tigers, 1908–21;
　　Washington Senators, 1921–23; manager, Washington Senators,
　　1923; Pittsburgh Pirates, 1927

• Carey, Max George "Scoops"—outfielder, Pittsburgh Pirates, 1910–
　　26; Brooklyn Robins, 1926–27

Carlson, Harold Gust "Hal"—right-handed pitcher, Pittsburgh Pirates,
　　1917–23; Philadelphia Phillies, 1924–27; Chicago Cubs, 1927

Carroll, Owen Thomas "Ownie"—right-handed pitcher, Detroit
　　Tigers, 1925, 1927

Carter, John Howard "Howie"—infielder, Cincinnati Reds, 1926

Coakley, Andrew James "Andy"—right-handed pitcher, Philadelphia
　　Athletics, 1902–06; Cincinnati Reds, 1907–08; Chicago Cubs,
　　1908–09; New York Yankees, 1911; baseball coach, Columbia
　　University Lions, 1915–27

• Cobb, Tyrus Raymond "Georgia Peach"—outfielder, Detroit Tigers,
　　1905–26; Philadelphia Athletics, 1927; manager, Detroit Tigers,
　　1921–26

• Collins, Edward Trowbridge, Sr., "Cocky"—second baseman,
　　Philadelphia Athletics, 1906–14, 1927; Chicago White Sox,
　　1915–26; manager, Chicago White Sox, 1924–26

---

* The baseball team that would one day be known as the Brooklyn Dodgers was
nicknamed the Robins in honor of manager Wilbert Robinson.

• Combs, Earle Bryan "Kentucky Colonel"—outfielder, New York
  Yankees, 1924–27

Connery, Bob—head scout, New York Yankees, 1918–24; president,
  American Association, 1925–27

Contente, Willie—schoolmate of Lou's when the Gehrig family lived
  on the 2200 block of Amsterdam Avenue

Coombs, John Wesley "Colby Jack"—right-handed pitcher,
  Philadelphia Athletics, 1906–14; Brooklyn Robins 1915–18;
  Detroit Tigers, 1920; manager, Philadelphia Phillies, 1919

• Crawford, Samuel Earl "Wahoo Sam"—outfielder, Cincinnati Reds,
  1899–1902; Detroit Tigers, 1903–17

Cvengros, Michael John "Mike"—left-handed pitcher, New York
  Giants, 1922; Chicago White Sox, 1923–25; Pittsburgh Pirates,
  1927

• Dreyfuss, Bernhard "Barney"—owner, Pittsburgh Pirates, 1900–27

Dugan, Joseph Anthony "Jumping Joe"—infielder, Philadelphia
  Athletics, 1917–21; Boston Red Sox, 1922; New York Yankees,
  1922–27

DuSchatko, Alfred—mathematics teacher and baseball coach,
  Commerce High School, 1916–17

Engel, Joseph William—left-handed pitcher, Washington Senators,
  1912–15, 1920; Cincinnati Reds, 1917; Cleveland Indians, 1919;
  scout, Washington Senators, 1920–27

• Evans, William George "Billy"—American League umpire, 1906–27

Falk, Bibb August "Jockey"—outfielder, Chicago White Sox, 1920–27

Farrell, Edward Stephen "Doc"—infielder, New York Giants, 1925–27;
  Boston Braves, 1927

• Frisch, Frank Francis "Fordham Flash"—infielder, New York Giants,
  1919–26; St. Louis Cardinals, 1927

Gazella, Michael—third baseman, New York Yankees, 1923, 1926–27

• Grimes, Burleigh Arland "Old Stubblebeard"—right-handed pitcher,
  Pittsburgh Pirates, 1916–17; Brooklyn Robins 1918–26; New
  York Giants, 1927

Haines, Henry Luther "Hinkey"—outfielder, New York Yankees, 1923; quarterback, New York Giants, National Football League, 1925–27

• Haines, Jesse Joseph "Pop"—right-handed pitcher, Cincinnati Reds, 1918; St. Louis Cardinals, 1920–27

Harris, Joseph "Moon"—first baseman, New York Yankees, 1914; Cleveland Indians, 1917, 1919; Boston Red Sox, 1922–25; Washington Senators, 1925–26; Pittsburgh Pirates, 1927

• Harris, Stanley Raymond "Bucky"—second baseman, Washington Senators, 1919–27; manager, Washington Senators, 1924–27

Haughton, Percy—football coach, Columbia University Lions, 1923–24

• Heilmann, Harry Edwin "Slug"—outfielder, Detroit Tigers, 1914, 1916–27

Hendrick, Harvey "Gink"—outfielder-infielder, New York Yankees, 1923–24; Cleveland Indians, 1925; Brooklyn Robins 1927

Hill, Carmen Proctor "Specs"—right-handed pitcher, Pittsburgh Pirates, 1915–16, 1918–19; New York Giants, 1922; Pittsburgh Pirates, 1926–27

Hofmann, Fred "Bootnose"—catcher, New York Yankees, 1919–25; Boston Red Sox, 1927

Hollingsworth, John Burnette "Bonnie"—right-handed pitcher, Pittsburgh Pirates, 1922; Washington Senators, 1923; Brooklyn Robins, 1924

• Hornsby, Rogers "Rajah"—second baseman, St. Louis Cardinals, 1915–26; New York Giants, 1927; manager, St. Louis Cardinals, 1925–26; New York Giants, 1927

• Hoyt, Waite Charles "Schoolboy"—right-handed pitcher, New York Giants, 1918; Boston Red Sox, 1919–20; New York Yankees, 1921–27

• Huggins, Miller James "Hug"—second baseman, Cincinnati Reds, 1904–09; St. Louis Cardinals, 1910–16; manager, St. Louis Cardinals, 1913–17; manager, New York Yankees, 1918–27

Johnson, Ernest Rudolph—shortstop, Chicago White Sox, 1912; St.
    Louis Browns, 1916–18; Chicago White Sox, 1921–23; New
    York Yankees, 1923–25

• Johnson, Walter Perry "Big Train"—right-handed pitcher, Washington
    Senators, 1907–27

Jones, Samuel Pond "Sad Sam"—right-handed pitcher, Cleveland
    Naps,* 1914; Cleveland Indians, 1915; Boston Red Sox, 1916–
    21; New York Yankees, 1922–26; St. Louis Browns, 1927

Judge, Joseph Ignatius "Joe"—first baseman, Washington Senators,
    1915–27

Kane, Harry—outfielder, Fordham University Rams, 1912–15;
    baseball coach, Commerce High School, 1918–27

Karow, Martin Gregory "Marty"—infielder, Boston Red Sox, 1927

Kauff, Benjamin Michael "Benny"—outfielder, New York
    Highlanders,† 1912; New York Giants, 1916–20

• Keeler, William Henry "Wee Willie"—outfielder, New York
    Giants, 1892–93; Brooklyn Bridegrooms, 1893; Baltimore
    Orioles, 1894–98; Brooklyn Superbas, 1899–1902; New York
    Highlanders, 1903–09; New York Giants, 1910

Koenig, Mark Anthony "Marcus Aurelius"—shortstop, New York
    Yankees, 1925–27

Koppisch, Walter Frederick—running back, Buffalo Bisons, National
    Football League, 1925; New York Giants, 1926

Kremer, Remy Peter "Ray"—right-handed pitcher, Pittsburgh Pirates,
    1924–27

Krichell, Paul Bernard—catcher, St. Louis Browns, 1911–12; coach,
    Boston Red Sox, 1919; scout, New York Yankees, 1920–24; head
    scout, New York Yankees, 1925–27

---

* The baseball team that would eventually be called the Cleveland Indians was
founded in 1903 and named the Napoleons, shortened to Naps.

† The New York Yankees originally were nicknamed the Highlanders since their
home stadium was built on some of the highest ground in Manhattan.

• Lazzeri, Anthony Michael "Tony"—second baseman, New York
  Yankees, 1926–27

• Lindstrom, Frederick Charles "Freddie"—third baseman, New York
  Giants, 1924–27

Lutzke, Walter John "Rube"—third baseman, Cleveland Indians,
  1923–27

• Mathewson, Christopher "Matty"—right-handed pitcher, New York
  Giants, 1900–16; Cincinnati Reds, 1916; manager, Cincinnati
  Reds, 1916–18

• McGraw, John Joseph "Mugsy"—third baseman, Baltimore Orioles,
  1892–99; St. Louis Cardinals, 1900; Baltimore Orioles,* 1901–
  02; New York Giants, 1902–06; manager, Baltimore Orioles,
  1899, 1901–02; New York Giants, 1902–27

McLaughlin, Albert—catcher, New York University Violets

McNally, Michael Joseph "Minooka Mike"—infielder, Boston Red
  Sox, 1915–20; New York Yankees, 1921–24; Washington
  Senators, 1925

Meadows, Henry Lee "Specs"—right-handed pitcher, St. Louis
  Cardinals, 1915–19; Philadelphia Phillies, 1919–23; Pittsburgh
  Pirates, 1923–27

Meusel, Robert William "Long Bob"—outfielder, New York Yankees,
  1920–27

Miljus, John Kenneth "Big Serb"—right-handed pitcher, Brooklyn
  Robins, 1917, 1920–21; Pittsburgh Pirates, 1927

Moore, William Wilcy "Cy"—right-handed pitcher, New York
  Yankees, 1927

Nehf, Arthur Neukom "Art"—left-handed pitcher, Boston Braves,
  1915–19; New York Giants, 1919–26; Cincinnati Reds, 1926–
  27; Chicago Cubs, 1927

---

* The team name referred to here is that of a short-lived American League team,
not the major-league Orioles of today.

Nevers, Ernest Alonzo "Ernie"—right-handed pitcher, St. Louis
  Browns, 1926–27
O'Connor, Patrick Francis "Paddy"—catcher, Pittsburgh Pirates,
  1908–10; St. Louis Cardinals, 1914; New York Yankees, 1918;
  coach, New York Yankees, 1918–19; manager, Hartford Senators
  [minor league], 1923–27
O'Leary, Charles Timothy "Charley"—shortstop, Detroit Tigers,
  1904–12; St. Louis Cardinals, 1913; coach, New York Yankees,
  1920–27
Overall, Orval "Orvie"—right-handed pitcher, Cincinnati Reds,
  1905–06; Chicago Cubs, 1906–13
Pease, George—running back, New York Yankees, American Football
  League, 1926
• Pennock, Herbert Jefferis "Squire of Kennett Square"—left-handed
  pitcher, Philadelphia Athletics, 1912–15; Boston Red Sox,
  1915–17, 1919–22; New York Yankees, 1923–27
Petty, Jesse Lee "Silver Fox"—left-handed pitcher, Cleveland Indians,
  1921; Brooklyn Robins 1925–27
Pipgras, George William "Great Dane"—right-handed pitcher, New
  York Yankees, 1923–24, 1927
Pipp, Walter Clement "Wally"—first baseman, Detroit Tigers, 1913;
  New York Yankees, 1915–25; Cincinnati Reds, 1926–27
Quinn, John Picus "Jack"—right-handed pitcher, New York
  Highlanders, 1909–12; Boston Braves, 1913; Chicago White
  Sox, 1918; New York Yankees, 1919–21; Boston Red Sox,
  1922–25; Philadelphia Athletics, 1925–27
Reulbach, Edward Marvin "Big Ed"—right-handed pitcher, Chicago
  Cubs, 1905–13; Brooklyn Superbas, 1913; Brooklyn Robins
  1914; Boston Braves, 1916–17
Rhyne, Harold J. "Hal"—infielder, Pittsburgh Pirates, 1926–27
• Rice, Edgar Charles "Sam"—outfielder, Washington Senators,
  1915–27

•Rixey, Eppa "Jeptha"—left-handed pitcher, Philadelphia Phillies,
   1912–17, 1919–20; Cincinnati Reds, 1921–27

Robertson, Davis Aydelotte "Davey"—outfielder, New York Giants,
   1912, 1914–17; Chicago Cubs, 1919–21; Pittsburgh Pirates,
   1921; New York Giants, 1922

Roderick, Ben—back, Canton Bulldogs, 1923, 1926, National
   Football League; Buffalo Bisons, 1927

Rowland, Clarence Henry "Pants"—American League umpire,
   1923–27

Ruel, Herold Dominic "Muddy"—catcher, St. Louis Browns, 1915;
   New York Yankees, 1917–20; Boston Red Sox, 1921–22;
   Washington Senators, 1923–27

Ruether, Walter Henry "Dutch"—left-handed pitcher, Chicago
   Cubs, 1917; Cincinnati Reds, 1917–20; Brooklyn Robins
   1921–24; Washington Senators, 1925–26; New York Yankees,
   1926–27

• Ruppert, Jacob "Colonel," Jr.—owner, New York Yankees, 1914–27

• Ruth, George Herman "Babe"—pitcher-outfielder, Boston Red Sox,
   1914–19; outfielder, New York Yankees, 1920–27

Ryan, Wilfred Patrick Dolan "Rosy"—right-handed pitcher, New
   York Giants, 1919–24; Boston Braves, 1925–26

Schacht, Alexander "Al"—right-handed pitcher, Washington Senators,
   1919–21

Schang, Walter Henry "Wally"—catcher, Philadelphia Athletics,
   1913–17; Boston Red Sox, 1918–20; New York Yankees,
   1921–25; St. Louis Browns, 1926–27

Scott, Lewis Everett "Deacon"—shortstop, Boston Red Sox, 1914–
   21; New York Yankees, 1922–25; Washington Senators, 1925;
   Chicago White Sox, 1926; Cincinnati Reds, 1926

Sewell, James Luther "Luke"—catcher, Cleveland Indians, 1921–27

Sewell, Joseph Wheeler "Joey"—shortstop, Cleveland Indians,
   1920–27

Shanks, Howard Samuel "Hawk"—infielder-outfielder, Washington
   Senators, 1912–22; Boston Red Sox, 1923–24; New York
   Yankees, 1925
Shawkey, James Robert "Bob"—right-handed pitcher, Philadelphia
   Athletics, 1913–15; New York Yankees, 1915–27
Sherdel, William Henry "Wee Willie"—left-handed pitcher, St. Louis
   Cardinals, 1918–27
Shocker, Urban James "Urb"—right-handed pitcher, New York Yankees,
   1916–17; St. Louis Browns, 1919–24; New York Yankees, 1925–27
• Sisler, George Harold "Gorgeous George"—first baseman, St. Louis
   Browns, 1915–27; manager, St. Louis Browns, 1924–26
Smith, Earl Sutton "Oil"—catcher, New York Giants, 1919–23;
   Boston Braves, 1923–24; Pittsburgh Pirates, 1924–27
• Speaker, Tristram E. "Spoke"—outfielder, Boston Americans,*
   1907; Boston Red Sox, 1908–15; Cleveland Indians, 1916–27;
   manager, Cleveland Indians, 1919–26
Spencer, Roy Hampton—catcher, Pittsburgh Pirates, 1925–27
Statz, Arnold John "Jigger"—outfielder, New York Giants, 1919–20;
   Boston Red Sox, 1920; Chicago Cubs, 1922–25; Brooklyn
   Robins, 1927
Stockder, Archibald—professor of business, Columbia University,
   1917–27
• Traynor, Harold Joseph "Pie"—third baseman, Pittsburgh Pirates,
   1920–27
Tunney, James Joseph "Gene"—heavyweight boxing champion,
   1926–27
Uhle, George Ernest "Bull"—right-handed pitcher, Cleveland
   Indians, 1919–27

---

* A team in the newly formed American League in 1901, the Boston franchise
officially adopted the name Americans until 1908, when it became known as the
Red Sox.

• Vance, Clarence Arthur "Dazzy"—right-handed pitcher, Pittsburgh
  Pirates, 1915; New York Yankees, 1915, 1918; Brooklyn Robins
  1922–27

Vangilder, Elam Russell—right-handed pitcher, St. Louis Browns,
  1919–27

• Waner, Lloyd James "Little Poison"—outfielder, Pittsburgh Pirates,
  1927

• Waner, Paul Glee "Big Poison"—outfielder, Pittsburgh Pirates,
  1926–27

Ward, Aaron Lee—second baseman, New York Yankees, 1917–26;
  Chicago White Sox, 1927

Whitehill, Earl—left-handed pitcher, Detroit Tigers, 1923–27

Williams, Fred "Cy"—outfielder, Chicago Cubs, 1912–17;
  Philadelphia Phillies, 1918–27

Wingard, Ernest James "Ernie"—left-handed pitcher, St. Louis
  Browns, 1924–27

Witt, Lawton Walter "Whitey"—infielder-outfielder, Philadelphia
  Athletics, 1916–17, 1919–21; New York Yankees, 1922–25;
  Brooklyn Robins 1926

Woods, Albert A. "Doc"—trainer, St. Louis Cardinals, 1913–17; New
  York Yankees, 1917–27

Wright, Forest Glenn "Buckshot"—shortstop, Pittsburgh Pirates,
  1924–27

• Youngs, Ross Middlebrook "Pep"—outfielder, New York Giants,
  1917–26

Lou Gehrig's Regular Season Lifetime Stats

YEAR	AGE	G	AB	H	2B	3B	HR	R	RBI	BB	SO	BA	EST. SALARY
1923	20	13	26	11	4	1	1	6	9	2	5	.423	$2,400
1924	21	10	12	6	1	0	0	2	5	1	3	.500	2,750
1925	22	126	437	129	23	10	20	73	68	46	49	.295	3,750
1926	23	155	572	179	47	**20**	16	135	112	105	73	.313	6,500
1927	24	**155**	584	218	**52**	18	47	149	**175**	109	84	.373	7,500
1928	25	154	562	210	**47**	13	27	139	**142**	95	69	.374	25,000
1929	26	154	553	166	32	10	35	127	126	122	68	.300	25,000
1930	27	**154**	581	220	42	17	41	143	**174**	101	63	.379	25,000
1931	28	155	619	**211**	31	15	**46**	**163**	**184**	117	56	.341	25,000
1932	29	**156**	596	208	42	9	34	138	151	108	38	.349	25,000
1933	30	152	593	198	41	12	32	**138**	139	92	42	.334	23,000
1934	31	**154**	579	210	40	6	49	128	**165**	109	31	**.363**	23,000
1935	32	149	535	176	26	10	30	**125**	119	**132**	38	.329	31,000
1936	33	155	579	205	37	7	49	**167**	152	**130**	46	.354	31,000
1937	34	157	569	200	37	9	37	138	159	**127**	49	.351	36,750
1938	35	157	576	170	32	6	29	115	114	107	75	.295	39,000
1939	36	8	28	4	0	0	0	2	1	5	1	.143	35,000
Totals		2,164	8,001	2,721	534	163	493	1,888	1,995	1,508	790	.340	

League-leading totals in bold

Lou Gehrig's Tips on How to Watch a Ball Game

The *Detroit Free Press* of June 2, 1940, featured an article titled "Meet Lou Gehrig," by columnist Jack Sher. The following tips on how to watch a baseball game—things to do, things to watch for, and things to avoid—appeared in conjunction with Sher's article, which included material from his last interview with Gehrig in his office on Centre Street. Sher remembered, "He was friendly and cheerful. He talked about baseball as though he were still playing it."

1. To properly enjoy the game, you should have a thorough knowledge of the playing rules, which can be bought in almost any book or sporting goods store.

2. Always follow the ball. I remember a game my wife and I were watching in Detroit. There was a man on second base with two out. The ball was hit to the outfield. Instead of following it, many of the fans, my wife included, were watching the runner on second, who had left to try and make home. But the man who had hit the ball—I think it was Goose Goslin—was trying to make second. The ball was thrown to second base, and had he been put out, the run would not have counted. By following the base runner instead of the ball, many of the fans missed the play.

3. You can enjoy the game more if you try to put yourself in the position of one of the players on the field or one of the managers of either team.

4. When there is an exciting moment on the diamond—for example, two men out and two on base—try to visualize all the possibilities of the situation while waiting for the pitcher to deliver the ball.

5. When a new batter comes to the plate, it's interesting to notice how the outfield and infield shift to play him. You can then tell what sort of batter he is.

6. It's interesting to notice the different attitude of players during a hot game. Some are excited, some very cool, and others seem to be half asleep. But most of the time, those who seem to be sleeping certainly fool you when the play starts.

7. Keep up on your baseball news in the newspapers and on the radio. You'll get more kick out of the game if you know the past performances of the various players.

8. When the umpire makes a decision, you may think him wrong. But, remember, he is well grounded in the rules of play. Keep in mind that in an argument between players and the umpire, the umpire is usually right. The player is prejudiced by his desire to win.

9. Don't be misled by the shouts and opinions of other spectators. Sometimes, from the shouts around you, it seems as if everything on the field is a mistake. It usually isn't. The cry you most often hear is "Balk." You hear it perhaps a hundred times, and during that time, the pitcher makes, perhaps, one balk.

Acknowledgments

There are three people who deserve recognition for Lou Gehrig's *Lost Memoir* reaching the public. First and foremost is my wife, Maureen, who has been with me every step as I transcribed Lou's manuscript, conducted research, and wrote the biographical essay. She has read every word in the various versions of our manuscripts and listened patiently as I joked repeatedly that Lou was a perfect coauthor: his assignments were always on time, he never complained about anything, and he never interrupted editorial meetings. That patience is undoubtedly why we have been married for more than fifty years.

Roger Williams, my esteemed agent at the Roger Williams Agency, has proven to be the perfect person for advancing my writing career to a new level. Roger's many years of experience in nearly all facets of the publishing world have convinced me that he is the best individual to guide my work from a manuscript to a completed book. When I first approached him with the Gehrig manuscript, Roger was naturally hesitant because the project just seemed too good to be true. I soon convinced him that Lou's memoir was the real thing, so his enthusiasm grew every time we talked.

Roger's passion for Lou's memoir resulted in him contacting

Stuart Roberts, senior editor at Simon & Schuster. Immediately realizing the potential for such a book, Stuart called me the following day to inquire about the manuscript. I knew we were beginning a harmonious relationship when Stuart and I spent more than five minutes discussing the writing of Robert Graves, whom we both admire. We both admitted that no such thing as a perfect manuscript existed, so as Lou's pages, along with my biographical essay, passed back and forth, there were no problems about questions, suggestions, or cutting extraneous material. I cannot imagine working with a finer editor.

Four people deserve recognition for their assistance in assembling the photograph array that accompanies this text. Michelle Press at Getty Images was charming and efficient in handling my large order. Susan Lennon at Alamy Images was pleasant and helpful in arranging the purchase of Lou Gehrig photographs from that amazing collection. Carla Reczek was the epitome of efficiency in retrieving photographs from the Ernie Harwell Sports Collection at the Detroit Public Library. Kudos also to John Horne at the National Baseball Hall of Fame Library who was instrumental in tracking down images of Lou Gehrig with his mother, and with Coach Pat O'Connor of the Hartford Senators.

Copy editor Phil Bashe deserves a special thank-you. In my other dozen or so books I have never had anyone who paid attention to every detail like Phil did in this manuscript. He is a true pro at his craft and I would love to have him work on any of my future book projects. I have no doubt that he will look at this short paragraph and make a few corrections or suggestions.

Lastly, I would like to thank my son, Don, also known as

Dr. Donald H. Gaff, associate professor of anthropology at the University of Northern Iowa. We have edited several books together over the past few years, but he wanted this project to be all mine. As I write this, he still has not read the manuscript. He has, however, been only a phone call away and ready to answer any question on any subject, but mostly computer related. As Maureen and I grow older, Don has become the rock upon whom we depend.

Notes

Introduction

3   *"He was simply"*: Oakland Tribune, August 15, 1927, 14.

4   *"For the past decade"*: Ibid.

4   *"not hitting home runs"*: Ibid., August 10, 1927, 15.

4   *"Lou Gehrig has been"*: Ibid., August 31, 1927, 12.

5   *"back on the job again"*: Ibid., September 2, 1927, 27.

6   *"The smack of a ball"*: Gehrig, "Home Run," 7.

7   *"immortal because somehow he managed to touch"*: Heyn, Twelve Sports Immortals, 32.

Early Years

105   *"I had two sisters"*: Brundidge, "Lou Gehrig Gives Baseball Full Credit," 3.

105   *"My mother and father"*: Baltimore Sun, November 19, 1939, Magazine, 2.

105   *"big-boned, strong"*: Lieb, "Life of Lou Gehrig," 5.

105   *"I don't pretend Lou"*: Ibid.

107   *"From the time Lou"*: Ibid., 6.

107   *"I was a poor kid"*: Baltimore Sun, November 19, 1939, Magazine, 2.

107   *"I wasn't old enough"*: Brundidge, "Lou Gehrig Gives Baseball Full Credit," 3.

108   *"kept one foot"*: New York Daily News, August 17, 1927, 30.

109   *"He was shy, timid"*: Lieb, "Life of Lou Gehrig," 6.

109   *"Early in life"*: Gallico, Lou Gehrig, 38–39.

109   *"a left-handed catcher"*: Ibid., 41.

110 *"No one who went"*: Ibid., 43.

110 *"embarrassed that he"*: Gehrig and Durso, *My Luke and I*, 37–38.

111 *"a poor performer"*: Gallico, *Lou Gehrig*, 45.

111 *"if you happened to play"*: Viola, *Lou Gehrig*, 19.

112 *"foolishness"*: Lieb, "Life of Lou Gehrig," 8.

113 *"The real Babe never"*: *New York Daily News*, June 28, 1920, 8.

Columbia University to Yankee Stadium

115 *"stubborn and bull-headed"*: Lieb, "Life of Lou Gehrig," 8.

115 *"freshmen who looked"*: Gallico, *Lou Gehrig*, 64–65.

115 *"being in the college"*: Ibid., 65.

115 *"He withdrew still"*: Ibid., 66.

116 *"wild enough nearly"*: Hubler, *Lou Gehrig*, 25

116 *"stop a ball"*: *Pampa (TX) Daily News*, February 14, 1950, 5.

116 *"seeing a lumbering, awkward"*: *Des Moines Tribune*, August 4, 1937, 1.

116 *"When there were no"*: *El Paso (TX) Times*, December 26, 1951, 19.

116 *"the worst thing they do"*: *New York Times*, September 28, 1963, 47.

117 *"I have seen him hit"*: *New York Daily News*, May 6, 1923, 61.

117 *"My dad hadn't worked"*: *Cleveland Plain Dealer*, June 3, 1941, 17.

118 *"Mom's been slaving"*: Lieb, "Life of Lou Gehrig," 10.

118 *"He was big"*: *Fort Lauderdale (FL) News*, March 22, 1955, 2.

119 *"a super world series"*: *Tampa Tribune*, April 19, 1923, 1.

119 *"He wanted players with spunk"*: *New York Daily News*, September 29, 1929, 73.

119 *"crab, a dour-faced"*: Ibid., September 26, 1929, 52.

119 *"bigger than baseball"*: Ibid., September 29, 1929, 73.

120 *"Huggins can't manage"*: Ibid., September 26, 1929, 54.

120 *"Gehrig would have"*: Lieb, "Life of Lou Gehrig," 12.

120 *"He warmed the bench"*: Hubler, *Lou Gehrig*, 31.

120 *"Never you mind, kid"*: Ibid., 32.

121 *"the slim, delicate lines"*: Ibid.

121 *"When he came here"*: Ibid., 36.

121 *"If someone had offered"*: Ibid., 37.

The Minors

122 *"the cold clinkers"*: Gallico, *Lou Gehrig*, 53.

122 *"elegance and ease"*: Ibid.

122 *"it tasted horrible"*: Ibid., 54.

123 *"What the hell"*: Ibid., 55–56.

123 *"one of the greatest"*: Hartford Courant, October 1, 1923, 9.

124 *"the Bambino's understudy"*: Ibid., October 7, 1923, Z2.

124 *"if he must go"*: Ibid., December 2, 1923, Z2.

124 *"They won't let me"*: New York Daily News, January 31, 1924, 25.

124 *"12 bucks in his pocket"*: Des Moines Tribune, August 4, 1937, 1.

125 *"The other Yankees"*: Gehrig and Durso, *My Luke and I*, 128–29.

125 *"highly skilled in the art"*: New York Daily News, March 19, 1924, 20.

125 *"It takes a lot of fuel"*: Tampa Bay Times, December 16, 1964, 37.

125 *"of the Ruthian variety"*: New York Daily News, March 6, 1924, 24.

126 *"They tried to break into"*: Ibid., March 30, 1924, 51.

126 *"a stunningly handsome"*: Gallico, *Lou Gehrig*, 65.

126 *"Shirley Temple's dimples"*: Hartford Courant, February 9, 1939, 17.

126 *"after a trial"*: Ibid., August 13, 1924, 14.

127 *"The baseball factories"*: Ibid., December 14, 1924, B2.

A Yankee Again

128 *"We got to get the team"*: Tampa Bay Times, March 5, 1950, 33.

128 *"I wonder whether"*: Ibid.

128 *"It isn't a game"*: Gallico, *Lou Gehrig*, 80–81.

128 *"they were the hardest"*: Ibid., 75–76.

129 *"drink, wench, and"*: Ibid., 79.

129 *"Those Yanks never"*: New York Daily News, October 5, 1930, 31.

129 *"a young, sincere giant"*: San Francisco Examiner, June 5, 1941, 21.

129 *"sincerely adored Ruth"*: Gallico, *Lou Gehrig*, 95.

129 *"The Babe's lusty love"*: Ibid.

129 *"If a guy flops"*: Windsor (Can.) Star, August 17, 1948, 12.

130 *"with the casual, carefree"*: Ibid.

130   *"gluttonously gorged himself"*: Ibid., October 17, 1948, 12.

130   *"green of face"*: Ibid.

131   *"It gave him his first"*: Boston Globe, September 30, 1938, 25.

131   *"some lime blew into"*: St. Louis Star-Times, July 18, 1941, 14.

131   *"While I was in the clubhouse"*: Madison (WI) Capitol Times, August 17, 1935, 7.

131   *"Do you want to get"*: Rochester (NY) Democrat and Chronicle, June 4, 1941, 23.

132   *"At the end of that time"*: St. Louis Star-Times, July 18, 1941, 14.

132   *"a rabble"*: Muncie (IN) Evening Press, July 5, 1950, 4.

132   *"Miller Huggins hasn't got"*: Ibid.

133   *"Put this on"*: Ibid.

133   *"Gehrig's tremendous breadth"*: New York Daily News, April 29, 1926, 30.

133   *"will make the Gotham fans"*: Brooklyn Daily Times, April 19, 1926, 14.

133   *"If you think I'm yellow"*: Hartford Courant, May 9, 1926, B3.

134   *"You told Whitehill"*: New York Daily News, May 9, 1926, 52.

134   *"stopping any kind of batted ball"*: Ibid., April 18, 1926, 38.

135   *"by seven furlongs"*: Ibid., October 3, 1926, 41.

Murderers' Row

136   *"Those fellows not only"*: Ann Arbor (MI) Daily, June 22, 1955, 3.

136   *"We never even worried"*: Passaic (NJ) Herald News, March 24, 2002, D2.

136   *"inspire awe"*: Appel, Pinstripe Empire, 151.

136   *"Gehrig was a smooth-faced"*: Frommer, Five O'Clock Lightning, 75.

137   *"honeyed epistles"*: New York Daily News, August 22, 1927, 25.

137   *"Although he had no trouble"*: Baton Rouge (LA) State-Times, September 1, 1987, 28.

137   *"somewhere in the vicinity"*: Minneapolis Tribune, August 14, 1927, Sports, 1.

137   *"There was no finer man"*: Tampa Tribune, October 23, 1985, 6.

137   *"That Gehrig, there was"*: Louisville (KY) Courier-Journal, June 8, 1958, 4, 1.

138   *"a flat failure"*: Minneapolis Tribune, August 7, 1927, Sports, 6.

138   *"My only thought is"*: Ibid.

138 "It seems to me": St. Louis Post-Dispatch, July 3, 1927, 1.

138 "Many a time": Brooklyn Daily Eagle, March 19, 1933, 33.

139 "carried an augur": Boston Globe, July 7, 1989, 35.

139 "could drink quite a": Ibid., July 18, 1982, 64.

139 "That'll cost you fifty bucks": Minneapolis Star Tribune, April 27, 1952, S6.

139 "Get a job on": Allentown (PA) Morning Call, June 7, 1928, 24.

140 "couldn't hit the water": Miami (FL) News, February 8, 1948, 9.

140 "Throw the batter off": Boston Globe, February 2, 1948, 4.

140 "Joe, I'm so scared": Ibid., December 2, 1943, 27.

140 "at the back of": Tampa Tribune, October 21, 1986, Sports, 6.

141 "used to doctor the ball": Elmira (NY) Star-Gazette, January 26, 1959, 12.

141 "I ain't a pitcher": Frommer, Five O'Clock Lightning, 29.

142 "They hear little and care less": Muncie (IN) Evening Press, July 21, 1930, 9.

142 "I was the weak sister": Cincinnati Enquirer, October 6, 1939, 12.

142 "A catcher is the wife": Allentown (PA) Morning Call, April 5, 1929, 33.

143 "weighty backstop": Detroit Free Press, March 1, 1931, 25.

143 "doesn't speak twenty-five words": Ibid.

143 "with unerring accuracy": Montreal (Can) Gazette, September 11, 1948, 19.

143 "a lanky, silent guy": New York Daily News, April 26, 1957, 25.

143 "I've seen Bob": Paterson (NJ) Morning Call, March 1, 1929, 35.

143 "in reaching their hotel": Quad-City (IA, IL) Times, October 2, 1935, 14.

145 "Easy living, easy money": Los Angeles Times, September 4, 1998, B9.

145 "God, we liked that": Cincinnati Enquirer, August 26, 1984, B18.

145 "He was a big, overgrown": Rockford (IL) Register Star, November 4, 1979, 90.

145 "Babe Ruth's suitcase": New York Daily News, December 19, 1961, 74.

145 "outside of baseball": Louisville (KY) Courier-Journal, October 11, 1976, D1.

145 "I don't think he": Rockford (IL) Register Star, November 4, 1979, 90.

145 "he did not have to": Boston Herald, August 16, 1973, 40.

145 "lucky hunch": Orlando (FL) Sentinel, January 18, 1935, 9.

145 "midget mascot": New York Daily News, January 17, 1935, 38.

146 "Them damn squirrels": Los Angeles Times, September 4, 1998, B9.

147 "He looked like a": Corpus Christi (TX) Times, February 2, 1976, B6.

147 "were toothpicks attached": San Francisco Examiner, February 9, 1944, 21.

147 "Sure, he drank": Richmond (IN) Palladium-Item, September 5, 1982, B1.

147 "even when he struck out": Rockford (IL) Register Star, November 4, 1979, 90.

147 "a circus with classical rhythm": Muncie (IN) Evening Press, April 5, 1944, 12.

148 "I played for the ball": San Francisco Examiner, October 22, 1927, 25.

148 "perhaps the most potent": Passaic (NJ) Herald News, March 24, 2002, D2.

148 "baseball's measuring stick": Elmira (NY) Star-Gazette, March 25, 2002, 5B.

148 "It's funny, but": Rochester (NY) Democrat and Chronicle, June 2, 1940, Magazine, 19.

That Storybook Season

149 "the strange human traffic": Cincinnati Enquirer, October 7, 1927, 1.

149 "A Ruth or a Gehrig": Austin (TX) American-Statesman, August 21, 1927, 7.

150 "It's like going from": Santa Ana (CA) Register, June 30, 1927, 19.

150 "right-handed hitter": New York Daily News, April 28, 1957, 26.

150 "there is always danger": Muncie (IN) Evening Press, April 26, 1927, 9.

150 "Death, pestilence and": St. Louis Star and Times, October 10, 1928, 16.

150 "Three men on": Harrisburg (PA) Evening News, June 3, 1941, 11.

151 "no matter how well": Ottawa (Can.) Journal, September 6, 1957, 23.

151 "mauve-tinted knickers": Brooklyn Standard Union, March 20, 1927, 16.

152 "got a kick out of": Gehrig and Durso, My Luke and I, 132.

152 "I felt like a tramp": Hubler, Lou Gehrig, 62.

152 "He came around here": Lincoln (NE) Evening Journal, July 6, 1927, 1.

152 "I try to keep": Hubler, Lou Gehrig, 63.

153 "ponderous home run": New York Daily News, May 17, 1927, 35.

153 "Sturdy as an oak": New York Daily News, June 19, 1927, 60.

154 "Somebody has given that bird": Elmira (NY) Star-Gazette, June 28, 1927, 9.

154 "a bad slump": San Francisco Examiner, October 22, 1927, 25.

155 "The home run pace": Ithaca (NY) Journal, September 24, 1927, 8.

155 "Even the home run race": Brooklyn Daily Times, September 14, 1927, 13.

155 *"They could no more"*: New York Daily News, October 1, 1927, 28.

155 *"Play ball!"*: New York Daily News, October 2, 1927, 67.

155 *"We came"*: Ibid.

156 *"Skin and clean the eels"*: Binghamton (NY) Press, August 16, 1927, 15.

156 *"that game would"*: Ibid.

156 *"Lou has always"*: Ibid.

157 *"to keep the damned things"*: Gehrig and Durso, My Luke and I, 130.

157 *"Da fans, dey planna"*: Brooklyn Daily Times, September 1, 1927, 47.

157 *"We've got a present"*: Louisville (KY) Courier-Journal, February 8, 1970, C2.

158 *"might just as well"*: Baton Rouge (LA) State-Times, September 1, 1987, 28.

158 *"Buster Gehrig flung"*: Baltimore Sun, October 4, 1927, 1.

159 *"The day before the Series"*: Boston Globe, September 30, 1938, 25.

159 *"Just lay the ball"*: Pittsburgh Post-Gazette, April 7, 1943, 14.

159 *"up against"*: Ibid.

159 *"sock-it-out-of-the-lot"*: New York Daily News, September 30, 1927, 63.

160 *"the hallmark of a boss pitcher"*: New York Daily News, October 7, 1927, 56.

160 *"How a championship"*: New York Daily News, October 7, 1927, 56.

160 *"Gehrig's fly"*: Ibid.

160 *"The Pirates didn't look"*: Wilmington Journal, September 28, 1960, 42.

161 *"Why, I heard some"*: Ibid.

161 *"as calm and cool"*: Pittsburgh Press, February 15, 1929, 33.

161 *"flung away his bat"*: New York Daily News, October 9, 1927, 67

161 *"Run, run, Wilcy!"*: Ibid., 66.

161 *"Moore's base hit"*: Ibid., 65.

161 *"showed a goofy streak"*: Ibid., 64.

162 *"It was like getting"*: Tampa Tribune, October 9, 1927, 2.

163 *"It was a Christmas"*: Allentown (PA) Morning Call, January 10, 1928, 19.

A Life Cut Short

164 *"Why should there be"*: Boston Globe, August 10, 1933, 19.

165 *"Lou, who had never"*: Gallico, Lou Gehrig, 118.

165 *"He might as well"*: Salt Lake Telegram, October 6, 1936, 16.

166 *"Lou Gehrig and a horse"*: Brooklyn Citizen, March 10, 1938, 6.

166 *"Gehrig was far and away"*: Des Moines Tribune, March 24, 1938, 5.

166 *"I have everything"*: Lieb, "Life of Lou Gehrig," 24.

166 *"he was underweight"*: Tampa Bay Times, December 30, 1956, 19.

167 *"You better look out"*: Binghamton (NY) Press and Sun-Bulletin, May 9, 1976, B6.

167 *"I was standing by"*: Tampa Bay Times, December 30, 1956, 19.

167 *"He would stumble"*: Gallico, Lou Gehrig, 14.

167 *"Judging strictly on appearance"*: New York Daily News, March 25, 1939, 60.

167 *"It was pure torture"*: Tampa Bay Times, December 30, 1956, 19

168 *"Right now, I can't"*: New York Daily News, March 30, 1939, 52.

168 *"He started to take"*: Gallico, Lou Gehrig, 15.

168 *"began to observe"*: Lieb, "Life of Lou Gehrig," 26.

168 *"If he were a rookie"*: New York Daily News, March 30, 1939, 52.

168 *"I knew something"*: Hartford Courant, August 10, 1939, 15.

168 *"They meant it to be"*: Lieb, "Life of Lou Gehrig," 28.

169 *"Gehrig is dead wood"*: Brooklyn Daily Eagle, May 1, 1939, 18.

169 *"The fans broke out"*: Danville (PA) News, May 4, 1959, 5.

170 *"The other night, I was"*: Hartford Courant, August 10, 1939, 15.

170 *"He was the most cheerful"*: Tampa Bay Times, December 30, 1956, 19.

170 *"Baseball reached the most dramatic"*: Cincinnati Enquirer, July 6, 1939, 12.

171 *"wasted ghost"*: Atlanta Constitution, December 14, 1943, 20.

171 *"Fans, for the past"*: New York Daily News, July 30, 1939, 35.

172 *"This was Gehrig's last"*: Cincinnati Enquirer, July 6, 1939, 11.

172 *"I thought I was"*: Montreal (Can.) Gazette, January 14, 1943, 16.

172 *"Did my speech"*: Elmira (NY) Star-Gazette, July 5, 1939, 15.

172 *"I don't want any"*: Rochester (NY) Democrat and Chronicle, October 10, 1939, 20.

173 *"I am through with baseball"*: New York Daily News, October 12, 1939, 4.

173 *"sports seem to give"*: Rochester (NY) Democrat and Chronicle, December 8, 1940, 24.

174 *"I handed him a cigarette"*: San Francisco Examiner, February 16, 1941, Sports, 5.

174 *"He was a hopeless figure"*: Tampa Tribune, June 3, 1941, 2.

174 *"I'm developing a pouch"*: Hagerstown (MD) Daily Mail, January 31, 1941, 8.

174 "his face started": Nashville Tennessean, June 3, 1941, 10.

174 "he never gained": Pittsburgh Sun-Telegraph, September 21, 1941, 27.

175 "As the disease progressed": Tampa Bay Times, May 10, 1949, 2.

175 "When I left him": Elmira (NY) Star-Gazette, June 4, 1941, 8

176 "You moved along": Ibid., 14.

Fading into History

177 "June 19, 1903": New York Daily News, July 7, 1941, 37.

179 "Natural strength, acquired skill": Victoria (TX) Advocate, April 25, 1943, 12.

179 "He'd complain that we": Gallico, Lou Gehrig, 8–9.

180 "4—Lou Gehrig": Rochester (NY) Democrat and Chronicle, January 27, 1942, 17.

180 "The Spirit of Lou Gehrig": New York Daily News, January 26, 1944, 26.

180 "there are about 50": Burlington (NC) Daily Times-News, May 13, 1942, 6.

180 "The one thing": Dayton (OH) Daily News, February 9, 1942, 14.

181 "a warm and gentle": Brooklyn Daily Eagle, July 16, 1942, 7.

182 "Why don't you write": Muncie (IN) Sunday Star, June 7, 1942, 10.

182 "This is the story": The Pride of the Yankees Program, July 15, 1942.

182 "Even though Lou": Brattleboro (VT) Daily Reformer, April 30, 1943, 2.

183 "I think Lou Gehrig": Nebraska State Journal (Lincoln, NE), October 3, 1943, 11.

184 "This may save a life": Odessa (TX) American, June 21, 1944, 6.

184 "He's gone, but to the": Nashville Tennessean, June 2, 1942, 8.

184 "The love that people had": Elmira (NY) Star-Gazette, June 23, 1941, 6.

184 "born under the shadow": Tampa Bay Times, June 12, 1942, 6.

185 "His life was gentle": New York Daily News, June 4, 1941, 58.

185 "Death had to take him sleeping": Tampa Bay Times, June 22, 1941, 15.

Lou Gehrig's Tips . . .

199 "Lou Gehrig's Tips": Detroit Free Press, June 2, 1940, Magazine, 6.

199 "He was friendly": Ibid.

Bibliography

Books and Articles

Appel, Marty. *Pinstripe Empire: The New York Yankees from Before the Babe to After the Boss.* New York: Bloomsbury USA, 2012.

Brundidge, Harry T. "Lou Gehrig Gives Baseball Full Credit for Rescuing Parents and Self from New York Tenement District." *Sporting News,* December 25, 1930, 3.

Bryson, Bill. *One Summer: America, 1927.* New York: Doubleday, 2013.

Carvalho, John P. *Frick*: Baseball's Third Commissioner.* Jefferson, NC: McFarland, 2016.

Castro, Tony. *Gehrig & the Babe: The Friendship and the Feud.* Chicago: Triumph Books, 2018.

Crampton, C. Ward. "Wham! He Hits It!" *Boys' Life* 27, no. 5 (May 1937), 18, 48–49.

Eig, Jonathan. *Luckiest Man: The Life and Death of Lou Gehrig.* New York: Simon & Schuster, 2005.

Frommer, Harvey. *Five O'Clock Lightning: Babe Ruth, Lou Gehrig, and the Greatest Baseball Team in History, the 1927 New York Yankees.* Hoboken, NJ: John Wiley and Sons, 2008.

Gallico, Paul. *Lou Gehrig, Pride of the Yankees.* New York: Grosset & Dunlap, 1942.

Gehrig, Eleanor, and Joseph Durso. *My Luke and I.* New York: Thomas Y. Crowell, 1976.

Gehrig, Lou. "Home Run." *Boys' Life* 19, no. 5 (May 1929), 7, 73–74.

Glueckstein, Fred. *The '27 Yankees.* Philadelphia: Xlibris, 2005.

Graham, Frank. *Lou Gehrig: A Quiet Hero.* Boston: Houghton Mifflin, 1969.

Heyn, Ernest V. *Twelve Sports Immortals.* New York: Bartholomew House, 1951.

Hubler, Richard G. *Lou Gehrig, The Iron Horse of Baseball.* Boston: Houghton Mifflin, 1941.

Levitt, Daniel R. *Ed Barrow: The Bulldog Who Built the Yankees' First Dynasty.* Lincoln: University of Nebraska Press, 2008.

Lieb, Fred. *Baseball as I Have Known It.* New York: Grosset & Dunlap, 1977.

Lieb, Frederick G. "Life of Lou Gehrig." In *Baseball Register.* St. Louis: C. C. Spink and Son, 1942.

Meany, Tom. *The Yankee Story.* New York: E. P. Dutton, 1960.

Robinson, Ray. *Iron Horse: Lou Gehrig in His Time.* New York: W. W. Norton, 1990.

Sandomir, Richard. *The Pride of the Yankees: Lou Gehrig, Gary Cooper, and the Making of a Classic.* New York: Hachette Books, 2017.

Sarnoff, Gary A. *The First Yankee Dynasty: Babe Ruth, Miller Huggins, and the Bronx Bombers of the 1920s.* Jefferson, NC: McFarland, 2014.

Steinberg, Steve. *The Colonel and Hug: The Partnership That Transformed the New York Yankees.* Lincoln: University of Nebraska Press, 2015.

Trachtenberg, Leo. *The Wonder Team: The True Story of the Incomparable 1927 New York Yankees.* Bowling Green, OH: Bowling Green State University, 1995.

Viola, Kevin. *Lou Gehrig.* Minneapolis: Lerner Sports, 2005.

Newspapers

Allentown (PA) Morning Call
Ann Arbor (MI) Daily
Atlanta Constitution
Austin (TX) American-Statesman
Baltimore Sun
Baton Rouge (LA) State-Times
Binghamton (NY) Press
Binghamton (NY) Press and Sun-Bulletin
Boston Globe
Boston Herald
Brattleboro (VT) Daily Reformer
Brooklyn Citizen
Brooklyn Daily Eagle
Brooklyn Standard Union
Burlington (NC) Daily Times-News
Cincinnati Enquirer
Cleveland Plain Dealer

Corpus Christi (TX) Times

Dayton (OH) Daily News

Des Moines Tribune

Detroit Free Press

El Paso (TX) Times

Elmira (NY) Post-Star

Elmira (NY) Star-Gazette

Fort Lauderdale (FL) News

Hagerstown (MD) Daily Mail

Harrisburg (PA) Evening News

Hartford Courant

Ithaca (NY) Journal

Lincoln (NE) Evening Journal

Los Angeles Times

Louisville (KY) Courier-Journal

Madison (WI) Capitol Times

Miami (FL) News

Minneapolis Star Tribune

Minneapolis Tribune

Montreal (Can.) Gazette

Muncie (IN) Evening Press

Muncie (IN) Sunday Star

Nashville Tennessean

Nebraska State Journal (Lincoln, NE)

New York Daily News

New York Times

Oakland Tribune

Odessa (TX) American

Orlando (FL) Sentinel

Ottawa (Can.) Journal

Pampa (TX) Daily News

Passaic (NJ) Herald News

Paterson (NJ) Morning Call

Pittsburgh Post-Gazette

Pittsburgh Press

Pittsburgh Sun-Telegraph

Quad-City (IA, IL) Times

Richmond (IN) Palladium-Item

Rochester (NY) Democrat and
   Chronicle

Rockford (IL) Register Star

Salt Lake Telegram

San Francisco Examiner

Santa Ana (CA) Register

St. Louis Post-Dispatch

St. Louis Star-Times

Tampa Bay Times

Victoria (TX) Advocate

Wilmington Journal

Windsor (Can.) Star

Illustration Credits

Courtesy of Ernie Harwell Sports Collection, Detroit Public Library: 1, 2, 18

Courtesy of Getty Images: 3, 4, 5, 8, 9, 10, 11, 12, 13, 14, 16, 17, 20, 21, 22, 23, 25, 26, 27, 28, 29

Courtesy of Alamy Images: 6, 19, 24

Courtesy of National Baseball Hall of Fame Library: 7, 15

Index

About the Author

Alan D. Gaff is an independent scholar and the author of several books of American Civil War and World War history, including *Bayonets in the Wilderness, Blood in the Argonne,* and *On Many a Bloody Field,* the latter hailed as "a masterpiece of Civil War scholarship" (*Bookwatch*). He lives in Indiana.